한류 팬에게 드리는 선물
최초의 한류 한글 · 영어 시집

한류연가

Hallyu Sonata

A gift for Hallyu fans all over the world
The first Korean-Wave(Hallyu) Poetry Book

한류 팬에게 드리는 선물
최초의 한류 한글·영어 시집

한류연가

초판 1쇄 인쇄 2025년 1월 10일

지은이	노단
발행인	박창재
편집/디자인	최평주, 박혜영
펴낸곳	도서출판 꼬레아우라
등록	2014. 10. 15.
등록번호	제 2014-000290 호
주소	서울시 강남구 언주로30길 10
전화	02-574-7300
팩스	02-572-0816
홈페이지	www.koreaura.net
전자우편	subs@koreaura.net
인쇄	네오프린텍 (주)
가격	20,000원

이 책의 저작권은 저자에게 있으며,
출판권은 도서출판 꼬레아우라에 있습니다.
Copyright©2025 Koreaura

ISBN 979-11-977778-5-1(03800)

한류 팬에게 드리는 선물
최초의 한류 한글·영어 시집

한류연가
Hallyu Sonata

A gift for Hallyu fans all over the world
The first Korean-Wave(Hallyu) Poetry Book

지은이 노단

도서출판 꼬레아우라
Koreaura Books

머리말

'한류시집'은 최고의 기념품

한류는 인류사에 제2의 르네상스를 연 신문명의 시작이다.

2002년 초에 방영된 TV드라마 <겨울연가>가 한류의 시작이었다면, 이제 한류는 세계문명사에 신 패러다임을 제시하고 있다. 지금 한류 팬은 세계 220개국에 2억 명에 달하고, 연간 500만 명 이상이 한국을 찾아온다.

한류는 K팝, 드라마, 영화, 연극, 의료, 건강, 관광, 음식, 장식품, 화장품, 교육, 유산, 게임, 주택, 웹툰을 포함하여 서비스산업의 전 분야로 확대되어 세계 문명에 새로운 기운을 불어넣어 주고 있다. 한류는 단순한 놀이문화가 아니라 서비스 콘텐츠산업의 새로운 영역이며, 이를 통해 소외와 불평등, 질병과 전쟁, 재해, 가난과 실업 등에 허덕이는 사람들에게 희망과 용기를 주고 있다.

지금 인천공항과 김포공항에서 공항철도로 쉽게 접근할 수 있는 홍대역 홍대거리에 가보면, 하루에 수만 명의 한류 관광객이 찾아와 이곳에서 한류 문화를 흡수하고 즐기며 기념품을 산다.

필자는 많은 경험과 강의, 그리고 영감을 통해 한류 문명의 본질과

현상에 관한 글을 써서 이 시집을 출간하게 되었다.

 이 책은 한류를 이해하려는 사람들에게 좋은 길잡이 겸 선물이 될 것이다. 특히 한류를 통해 한글을 배우려는 사람들에게 유익한 정보와 재미를 주는 문학 서적이 될 것이다.

2024년 가을, 서울 홍대거리에서

작가 노단 씀

Preface

"Korean Wave Poetry Book" is the best souvenir

The Korean Wave is the beginning of a new civilization that has opened a second renaissance in human history.

The TV drama 'Winter Sonata', which aired in early 2002 was the beginning of the Korean Wave, and now the Korean Wave is presenting a new paradigm for world civilization. Now, the number of Hallyu fans reaches 200 million in 220 countries around the world, and more than 5 million people visit Korea annually.

The Korean Wave has expanded to all sectors of the service industry, including K-pop, drama, film, theater, medical care, health, tourism, food, ornaments, cosmetics, education, Inheritance, games, housing, and webtoons, bringing new energy to global civilization.

The Korean Wave is not just a play culture, but a new area of the service content industry, giving hope and courage to those struggling with alienation, inequality, disease, war, disasters and poverty and unemployment.

If you go to Hongdae Street at Hongik University Station, which is easily accessible by airport railroad from Incheon Airport and Gimpo Airport, tens of thousands of Hallyu tourists come a day to absorb, enjoy, and buy souvenirs here.

Through a lot of experience, lectures, and inspiration, I wrote about the nature and phenomenon of Korean Wave civilization and published this collection of poems.

This book will be a good guide and gift for those who want to understand the Korean Wave. In particular, it will become a literary book that gives useful information and fun to those who want to learn Hangeul through the Korean Wave.

the autumn of 2024, on Hongdae Street in Seoul
written by Rohdan

목차

머리말   006
'한류시집'은 최고의 기념품

1장 ········ 015
BTS는 시대의 영웅
BTS의 메시지
BTS의 팬덤 ARMY
BTS의 노블레스 오블리주
BTS의 'Yet to Come'
BTS는 세계적인 엔터테이너
BTS의 'Lost'

2장 ········ 033
홍대거리가 부른다
홍대 입구 스케치
홍대거리는 열린 광장
홍대로 연가(HongDae Avenue Sonata)
홍대거리의 콘텐츠
사랑으로 충만한 거리
한류 문화의 지중해
큰 세상을 그리는 사람들

3장 ······· 053

한류의 바탕은 옳은 정신
한국인에게는 정이라는 독특한 에너지가 있다
한국의 좋은 기후와 한류
한국은 세계 식물공원
한류는 오랜 역사의 산물
한류는 인류몽(人類夢)을 꿈꾼다
한류의 혼(魂 Spirit)
한류의 흥(興 Fun)
한류의 멋(態 Elegance)
한류의 맛(味 Taste)

4장 ······· 079

장(醬)의 노래
한류와 유목주의(Nomadism)
한국인의 자연 친화적인 삶
백남준(白南準)을 아시나요?
한류 3.0시대
한국인의 신심(信心)
한류는 신인류가 완성한다
한류 문명의 사명

목차

5장 ······· 101

한국은 어떤 나라인가?
불행을 극복한 한국인
한국은 부지런한 아침의 나라
한국의 성공 배경
한국 현대사의 두 위대한 지도자
한글(韓㐉, Hangeul) 찬가
한글은 세계 최고의 표음문자
K-콘텐츠의 확대

6장 ······· 121

노래 아리랑(我理朗)의 참뜻
아모르 파티(Amor Fati)
곤경에 빠진 나를 구하는 지혜
멍때리기의 힘
멍때리기 수련 10가지
숨비소리
지푸라기

부록 / 한글 시 감상 141

들꽃 인생

사랑의 힘

아내의 기도

사당역 나그네

한국의 국기인 태극기는 건곤감리(乾坤坎離)의 철학을 담고 있다.
그것은 하늘과 땅, 물과 불을 상징하는 주역(周易)의 4개 괘(卦)이다.
The Taegeukgi, the national flag of Korea, contains the philosophy of Gun-Gon-Gam-Ri. They are four divinations which symbolizes heaven and earth, water and fire from the Book of Changes

1장

BTS는 시대의 영웅

BTS의 메시지

BTS의 팬덤 ARMY

BTS의 노블레스 오블리주

BTS의 'Yet to Come'

BTS는 세계적인 엔터테이너

BTS의 'Lost'

BTS는 시대의 영웅

한국인은 세 명이 걸어가면 노래를 흥얼거리지.
5,000만 국민의 최애곡(最愛曲) 18번은 '아리랑'이야.
그래서 세계 최초로 '노래방 문화'를 만들었고,
전국 5만 3천 개의 노래방에서 쉼 없이 노랫소리가 울려 퍼지지.
일 년 내내 노래경연대회가 열리는 흥이 넘치는 나라.

70년대에 백남준이 비디오 아트라는 새로운 예술을 개척하면서
한국문화는 세계 문화 시장으로 나아가기 시작했어.
백남준은 인류사에 제2의 르네상스의 실마리를 연 인물이지.
중세에 지중해 크레타섬을 중심으로 일어난
제1 르네상스에 버금하는 제2 르네상스의 출발 국이 한국이야.

BTS가 출현한 것은 결코 우연이 아니야.
6.25 전쟁 이후, 폐허에서 살아남기 위한 몸부림이
노래에서부터 불타기 시작하여 국민에게 희망과 용기를 주었지.
BTS는 영국의 비틀스에 이은 위대한 대박(大樸) 보컬이야.
세계 대중음악은 BTS 이전과 이후로 구분되기 시작하지.

한류 문화의 세계화에 크게 이바지한 BTS는
세계 현대사의 위대한 영웅들이고,
세계 음악사와 문명사에 대변혁을 불러온 선도자들이지.
BTS는 한류를 세계로 전파한 전도사들이야.

BTS is a hero of the times

When three Koreans walk, they hum a song.
50 million people's favorite song No. 18 is "Arirang."
So they created the world's first Karaoke culture,
The song is constantly played in 53,000 karaoke rooms across the country.
A country full of excitement where singing contests are held all year round.

In the 70s, Paik Nam-jun pioneered a new art called video art.
Korean culture is starting to move toward the global cultural market.
Paik Nam-jun is a person who opened the thread of a second renaissance in human history.
In the Middle Ages, the island of Crete in the Mediterranean Sea Korea is the starting point of the second Renaissance, which is comparable to the first one.

It's no coincidence that BTS appeared.
After the Korean War, the struggle to survive in ruins
It started to burn from the song and gave hope and courage to the people.
BTS is the great vocalist after the Beatles in England.

World pop music begins to distinguish between before and after BTS.

BTS, who contributed greatly to the globalization of Hallyu culture.
The great heroes of modern world history.
They are the leaders who revolutionized the history of world music and civilization.
BTS are evangelists who spread the Korean Wave around the world.

Seven members of BTS are greeting countless fans.

BTS의 메시지

BTS의 춤과 노래는 세련되고 정교하고,
에너지가 펄펄 넘치는 종합예술이지.
이제까지 세계인들이 보지 못한 놀라운 문화의 탄생이야.

BTS의 음악과 춤은 한국인의 DNA 속에 잠재된
재주와 흥이 발휘된 것이야.
그래서 서구 음악과는 다른 리듬, 메시지가 담겨 있지.
또 BTS의 노래에는 소망의 메시지가 가득해.
깊은 의논, 설득과 호소, 감동과 공감, 타협의 내용들이야.

중세 유럽인들은 동양 문명에 자극받아
고대 그리스, 로마 문명의 부흥 운동을 일으켰어.
인간 중심(人間中心)의 정신을 되살리려 한 것이지.
서구인들이 자만(自慢)에서 깨어났다는 얘기야.

그런데 지금 제2의 르네상스 같은 문화의 대전환을
바로 BTS가 시작한 것이야.
세계 2억 명에 달하는 아미(ARMY)가 그들과 하나가 됐지.

Messages from BTS

BTS's dance and songs are sophisticated and precise,
It's a comprehensive art that's full of energy.
It's the birth of an amazing culture that people around the world have never seen before.

BTS's music and dance are hidden in the DNA of Koreans
It's a show of dexterity and excitement.
So it has a different rhythm and message than Western music.
Also, BTS' songs are full of messages of hope.
It is also about deep discussion, persuasion and appeal, emotion and empathy, and compromise.

Medieval Europeans were inspired by Eastern civilization
Ancient Greece, which led to the revival of Roman civilization.
It was to revive the spirit centered on humans.
In other words, Westerners have woken up from complacency.

But now, we're going to see a cultural transformation like the second Renaissance
That's exactly what BTS started.
The world's 200 million ARMYs have become one with them.

BTS의 팬덤 ARMY

BTS의 팬들은 BTS의 성공적인 활동을 도왔어.
한국 가수 최초로 그래미 어워즈에서 공연하고,
히트 싱글 '다이너마이트'로
빌보드 핫 100 차트 1위를 차지하는 등
성공을 거두는 데 큰 도움을 주었어.
또한 아미는 K-팝을 전 세계에 알리고,
독특한 사운드와 스타일을 홍보하는 데 기여했어.

BTS의 팬덤 ARMY는 음악 산업을 넘어 전 세계에 영향을 미쳤어.
사회적 대의에 대한 행동주의와 헌신에 앞장서고 있지.
BTS는 정신 건강, 자기애, 사회 정의를 고창했고,
ARMY도 이런 큰 뜻을 위해 노력해 왔어.

팬들은 재난구호 기금 모금, 교육 이니셔티브 지원과 같은
자선 프로젝트를 조직했고,
흑인의 생명 존중 운동, 반아시아 인종 차별 반대 운동 등
정치적 대의를 지지하여 크게 결속했어.
이런 정신은 바로 한국인의 삶의 모토인 홍익인간과 같아.
2018년 BTS는 UN과 함께 '러브 유어셀프' 캠페인을 진행했지.
이 캠페인이 큰 성공을 거두어 BTS는 유엔 총회에서 연설한
최초의 케이팝 아티스트가 되었어.

BTS' fandom ARMY

BTS' fans helped them with their successful activities.
BTS is the first Korean singer to perform at the Grammy Awards,
They helped greatly in their success, topping the Billboard Hot 100 chart with their hit single "Dynamite."
ARMY also introduces K-pop to the world,
They contributed to promoting unique sounds and styles.

BTS' fandom ARMY has influenced the world beyond the music industry.
They are also leading the way in activism and commitment to social causes.
BTS advocated mental health, self-love, and social justice,
ARMY has been working towards this big meaning too.

Fans have organized charity projects such as raising funds for disaster relief and supporting educational initiatives,
Black Lives Matter Campaign, Anti-Asian Racism Campaign, etc
They were very united in support of the political cause.
This spirit is like Hongik human, the motto of Korean life.
In 2018, BTS ran a 'Love Yourself' campaign with the UN.
The campaign was a huge success, making BTS the first K-pop artist to speak at the U.N. General Assembly.

BTS의 노블레스 오블리주

BTS의 구성원 7명은 '5애정신(五愛精神)'이 투철해.
나라를 위해 모두 군 복무를 하는 애국정신,
한겨레의 역사, 문화, 전통을 사랑하는 애족정신,
시민과 ARMY를 사랑하고 봉사하는 애민정신,
자신들이 소속된 직장에 대한 강한 애사정신,
음악과 예술에 대한 애업정신이 훌륭해.

한국은 북한 공산집단과 대치 중이라서
모든 국민은 병역의 의무를 진다.
남자는 20세가 되면 18개월 동안 군에 복무하여
자기의 생명을 국가와 국민을 위해 바친다.
BTS는 세계적인 명망 보컬이지만,
주저 없이 전선으로 달려가
국가를 지키고 국민을 보호하고 있어.
자유 민주시민으로서 준법의식이 투철하여
모든 국민, ARMY로부터 칭송을 받고 있어.

BTS' noblesse oblige

The seven members of BTS are full of "Five Loves."
Patriotic spirit that all serve in the military for the country,
The spirit of loving the history, culture, and traditions of the Korean people,
The spirit of love for the people who love and serve citizens and ARMY,
They have a strong sense of love for the workplace they belong to,
The spirit of love for music and art is excellent.

South Korea is confronting North Korea's communist group
All citizens are obliged to serve in the military.
When a man turns 20, he'll serve in the military for 18 months
Dedicate one's life to one's country and people.
BTS is a world-renowned vocalist,
Without hesitation, run to the front.
They are protecting the country and protecting the people.
As liberal democratic citizens, they have a strong sense of compliance.
All the people, ARMYs, are praising them.

BTS의 'Yet to Come'

BTS는 전 세계 청소년들을 감성으로 묶는 데 성공했어.
'사랑의 공력(功力)'으로 인류에 큰 영향을 미쳤어.
이제는 감성주의에서 행동주의(activism)로 활동 포맷을 이전,
'인류몽'의 실천을 위해 행동하는 전위(the vanguard)가 돼야 해.

전쟁 종식과 평화, 인종 차별,
삶의 질과 빈곤, 마약 퇴치,
지구환경 보존, 기후, 우주와 해양쓰레기,
생명 존중과 인권의 신장, 문화예술의 발전,
역사 바로 세우기와 유물 주인 되찾아 주기 등에 앞장설 거야.
BTS는 민간 유엔(United Civilian)으로서 선한 영향력을 발휘,
전 세계 아미들의 요구에 부응해야지.

글로벌리즘에서 한 단계 나아가
로컬리즘과 내셔널리즘을 합한 글로커니즘(glocanism)으로,
활동의 질을 리포맷하고 폭을 넓혀야 해.
BTS의 진짜 도약은 이제부터야.
'Yet to Come.' 최고의 순간은 아직 오지 않았어.

BTS's 'Yet To Come'

BTS succeeded in binding teenagers around the world with emotions.
The power of love's success has had a huge impact on humanity.
Now, we're moving the format from emotionalism to activism,
BTS should be the vanguard who acts for the practice of 'human dreams.'

End of war, peace, racism, quality of life, poverty, drug eradication,
Conservation of the global environment, climate, space and marine waste,
Respect for life and the advancement of human rights, the development of culture and arts,
They will take the lead in establishing history and reclaiming the owner of the relics.
BTS exerts a good influence as a civilian United Nations,
Of course, they should meet the needs of ARMYs around the world.

Going one step further from globalism

Glocanism, a combination of localism and nationalism,
We need to reformat the quality of our activities and broaden them. BTS' real leap from now on.
"Yet to Come."
The best moment is yet to come.

BTS는 세계적인 엔터테이너
(TIME ; Entertainment of The Year ; BTS(2020) Person of the Year)

BTS는 세계에서 가장 큰 밴드가 됐다.
BTS는 여러 앨범을 내며 모든 종류의 기록을 깼고,
팝스타 반열의 정점에 올랐다.
BTS와 아미(ARMY) 사이의 유대는 코로나 팬데믹 속에서
더욱 깊어졌다. BTS는 세상이 멈추고,
사람들이 연결된 상태를 유지하려 분투한 시기에 그것을 해냈다.
고통과 냉소가 가득한 시대에 그들은 친절, 연결,
자기 포용이라는 메시지에 충실했다.
그 팀은 진정한 커뮤니티를 구축했고,
팬덤은 BTS의 긍정 메시지를 세계로 전파하고 있다.

BTS의 엄청난 성공은 팬덤의 위력과
음악의 소비 방식에 있어 거대한 변화를 말해주는 선례이다.
인종 차별 반대 캠페인 BLM(Black Lives Matter·흑인의 목숨도
소중하다)에 100만 달러를 기부함으로써,
BTS는 음악 산업에서 인간적 유대의 영향력을 보여주는 학습 사례이다.

BTS is a world-class entertainer

(TIME ; Entertainment of The Year ; BTS(2020) Person of the Year)

BTS became the best band in the world.

BTS broke all kinds of records by releasing several albums and reached the peak of their pop star ranks.

The bond between BTS and ARMY deepened amid the COVID-19 pandemic. BTS did it at a time when the world stopped, and people struggled to stay connected.

In an era full of pain and cynicism, they were true to the message of kindness, connection, and self-embracement.

The team has built a true community, and the fandom is spreading BTS' positive messages around the world.

The enormous success of BTS is a precedent that represents a huge change in the power of fandom and the way music is consumed.

By donating $1 million to Black Lives Matter(BLM), an anti-racism campaign,

BTS is a learning example of the influence of human ties in the music industry.

BTS의 'Lost'

남의 발자국만 따라가지 마.
그것은 안전하고 쉽지만,
새 길을 개척할 수는 없어.
큰 성공을 거둘 수가 없어.
세상에 우연이나 행운은 없어,
수많은 시행착오가 주는 가치야.
누구에게나 무명 시절은 있어.

'어디로 가는 개미를 본 적 있어?
단 한 번에 길을 찾는 법이 없어,
길을 잃는다는 건 그 길을 찾는 방법,
수없이 헤매도 난 나의 길을 믿어볼래.'

BTS' song, 'Lost'

Don't just follow other people's footsteps.
It is safe and easy, but,
You can't make a new path.
You can't achieve much success.
There's no chance or luck in the world,
It's the value of a lot of trials and errors.
Everyone has a time of obscurity.

Have you ever seen an ant going anywhere?
There's no way to find your way at once,
Getting lost is how to find your way,
I'll believe in my path, no matter how many times I've spent.

무궁화(無窮花, Hibiscus syriacus, Rose of Sharon)는 한국의 나라꽃으로서 '궁핍없이 오래가는 꽃'으로 해석되며, 이는 궁핍한 생활 없이 풍족하고 행복하게 오래 살고자 하는 한민족의 바람이 담겨져 있다.
Mugunghwa (Hibiscus syriacus, Rose of Sharon) is a Korean national flower and is interpreted as a 'long-lasting flower without poverty,' which contains the Korean people's desire to live a long and prosperous life without poverty.

2장

홍대거리가 부른다

홍대 입구 스케치

홍대거리는 열린 광장

홍대로 연가(HongDae Avenue Sonata)

홍대거리의 콘텐츠

사랑의 거리

한류 문화의 지중해

큰 세상을 그리는 사람들

홍대거리가 부른다

아무튼 가보자.
누군가 나를 기다릴 것 같은 그곳,
수만 리 먼 데서도 들리는 이 부름의 정체는
태초에 꿈꾸었던 꿈의 세상인가.
문화의 에덴동산인가.
사랑과 낭만 그리고 기쁨이 충만한 거리를 찾아가
나의 원초적인 그리움을 채색해보자.

인간의 간절한 욕구를 갈무리해주는
잔잔히 흐르는 문화의 외침을 함께 들어보자.
그리고 하나가 되어 온몸으로 부딪치며 느껴보자.
그곳,
한국 서울의 홍대거리는 그냥 스치는 길이 아니다.
행복과 구원을 더듬는 수행의 작은 광장,
젊음의 미래가 호흡하는 대박의 스폿(spot)이다.

HongDae Street is calling

Anyway, let's go.
Where I feel like someone will wait for me,
I can hear this call from tens of thousands of miles away
Is this the dream world you dreamed of in the beginning.
Is it the Garden of Eden of Culture.
Go to a street full of love, romance, and joy
Let's color my original longing.

It takes care of the desperate needs of us
Let's listen to the cry of a calm culture together.
And let's become one and feel it by hitting it with your whole body.
There,
Hongdae Street in Seoul is not just a passing road.
A small square of meditation that stammers for happiness and salvation,
The future of youth is the best spot to breathe.

홍대 입구 스케치

서울 지하철 홍대입구역에 내려
3번 출구 연남동 방면,
4번 출구 AK플라자 방면으로 나가면,
도도히 움직이는 아름다운 인파(人波)를 만난다.
큰 도로를 사이에 두고 펼쳐진 풍광이 조금 다르지만,
K-culture의 참모습이 가득한 거리이다.
멈춤과 둘러봄의 여유.
발견의 기쁨과 웃음,
이색문물의 구경과 쇼핑,
그리고 천천히 음미하며 움직이는 사람들.

세계 각국에서 모여든 사람들이
소곤거리며 위에서 아래로, 아래에서 위로
큰길에서 골목길로 손에 손잡고 흘러든다.
순전히 색색의 맑은 물결,
인종도, 성별도, 스타일도 각기 다른 사람들,
흥미 가득한 인간 원초의 욕망이 흐른다.

아무도 남의 눈을 의식할 필요가 없는 곳.
영어, 중국어, 일어, 베트남어, 태국어, 스페인어,
러시아어, 몽골어, 아랍어 등이 통용된다.

HongDae entrance sketch

Get off at Hongik University Station
Exit 3 toward Yeonnam-dong,
If you go out to exit 4 toward AK Plaza,
Meet the waves of beautiful people that move with pride.
The scenery spread out across the main road is a little different,
It is a street full of K-culture.
the leeway of stopping and looking around.
The joy and laughter of discovery,
The sightseeing and shopping of exotic culture,
And slowly savoring people.

People from all over the world
whispering from top to bottom, from bottom to top
It flows hand in hand from the main road to the alleyway.
a clear wave of pure color,
People of different races, genders, styles,
The desire of the original human being, full of interest, flows.

A place where no one has to be conscious of other people's eyes.
English, Chinese, Japanese, Vietnamese, Thai, Spanish,
Russian, Mongolian, and Arabic are spoken.

홍대거리는 열린 광장

친절하고 호기심 강하고 활기찬 한국인들이
노래와 춤, 영화, 드라마로 세계인을 즐겁게 한다.
'시작이 곧 반'이라는 한국인의 심성이
홍대거리에 오면 뭐든 시작하게 자극을 준다.

사진을 찍고, 예쁜 기념품을 사고,
버스 킹 가수 앞에 앉아 노래를 듣고,
풍광 좋은 곳에서 맛난 음식을 먹는다.
길가의 벤치에 앉아 이국(異國)의 문화를 만끽하는 사람들
그 인파 속에는 공통된 단어가 숨 쉰다.
'한류(韓流)'라고 부르는 신문명의 패러다임이 율동한다.
그 기운을 느끼고 맛보고 품에 안고,
새 희망과 용기를 얻으려고 오가는 사람들이
아름다운 인파를 만든다.

1,000여 개의 가게마다 따뜻한 정감과 미소가 가득하다.
열려있는 문으로 그냥 들어가면 되는 가게들,
차도 사람도 양보와 절제가 흐르는 신인류의 강.
21세기 중반에 열린 세계적인 문화장터,
신르네상스 문명이 탄생하는 곳.
인간답게 살아가는 방식을 함께 주고받는 열린 광장이다.

HongDae Street is an open square

Kind, curious, and energetic Koreans,
It is entertaining with songs, dances, movies, and dramas.
"The beginning is half." The Korean mentality
When you come to Hongik University Street, you give impetus to anything to start with.

Take pictures, buy pretty souvenirs,
Listen to songs sitting in front of a busking singer,
Eat delicious food in a scenic place.
people sitting on benches by the side of the road enjoying the culture of foreign countries
A common word breathes in the crowd.
The paradigm of a new civilization called "Korean Wave" moves.
Feel the energy, taste it, and hold it in your arms.
People who come and go for new hope and courage
It makes a beautiful crowd.

Every 1,000 stores is filled with warm feelings and smiles.
The stores that you can just enter through the open door,
The river of the new human race, where cars, people, and concessions and moderation flow.
A world-class cultural marketplace opened in the mid-21st

century, where the neo-Renaissance civilization is born.
It is an open square where people exchange ways to live like humans.

There are various shops in Hongdaero, which invite Hallyu tourists.

홍대로 연가(HongDae Avenue Sonata)

K-pop이 뭐 길래, 세계 젊은이들이 이리 요란이지?
어떻게 서울의 홍대거리가 젊은이들의 핫스폿(hot spot),
신문명의 메카가 된 거지?
오늘도 서울 홍대로에는 한류 관광객이 붐빈다.

홍대거리에 아름다운 밤의 커튼이 드리우면,
여행객의 눈마다 색색의 등불이 켜진다.
고단했던 일상, 흔들렸던 자존감이 활활 타오른다.
이곳에서는 배려와 양보 그리고 화합의 지혜가 번득인다.

홍대거리의 모든 가게에는 열정과 스토리의 기운이 있다.
사람들은 좋은 물건을 사지만,
그들은 열정과 사랑, 감동 그리고 미래를 여는 스토리를 산다.

우리는 홍대거리에서 새로운 인류 역사의 약동을 본다
그리고 진정한 만남의 꿈을 이룬다.
걸으면서 대화하고, 차를 마시며 영혼을 교감한다.
80억 인류 중에 참된 벗을 만나서 사귀고,
태초에 역사를 연 문화의 가치를 확인하며
우리는 떠오르는 제2 르네상스의 새로운 문명을 흡수한다.

Hongdae Avenue Sonata

What is K-pop, why are young people all over the world so loud? How can Hongdae Street in Seoul be a hot spot for young people,
It's become a mecca for the new civilization, right?
Hongdae Street in Seoul is also crowded with Hallyu tourists today.

If the beautiful night curtains are hung on Hongdae Street,
Colorful lanterns are lit in every traveler's eyes.
The tired daily life and the shaken self-esteem are blazing.
Here, the wisdom of consideration, concession, and harmony is shining.

Every store on Hongdae Street has the energy of passion and story. People buy good things, They buy passion, love, emotion and stories that open up the future.

We see a new leap in human history on Hongik University Street. And fulfills the dream of a true meeting.
Talking while walking, drinking tea and communicating with the soul. Meet a true friend out of 8 billion human beings and make a relationship,
It identifies the value of the culture that opened history in the beginning
We absorb the new civilization of the Second Renaissance that emerges.

홍대거리의 콘텐츠

인천국제공항에서 35분,
김포국제공항에서 15분,
공항철도를 타고 달리면 홍대역에 도착하지.
홍대역은 공항철도와 지하철 2호선이 닿는 곳.

홍대거리는 한류가 가득한 곳이야.
음악, 음식, 영화, 연극, 패션, 화장품, 의료, 장신구, 라이브공연,
골목골목 구석구석마다 한류 문화(K-Culture)가 가득해.
비슷한 것 같지만 색다른 맛과 멋, 음과 색이 충만해.
그리고 무엇보다 젊음의 열정이 가득한 곳.
세계 각국의 젊은이들이 만나고 교류하는 곳
수많은 이질문화가 한데 모여 융합하는 문화의 성지.
그래서 세계 각지에서 한류팬과 팬덤이 찾아오지.

홍대거리 서쪽에는 한반도를 가로지르는 한강이 흐르고,
반경 20km 안에 경복궁과 창경궁, 광화문, 남산, 청와대,
대통령실, 서울역, 이태원 국제거리가 있어.
연세대, 이화여대, 서강대, 경기대, 동국대, 추계예술대가
있고. 월드컵경기장과 공원, 하늘공원, 동대문시장,
남대문시장이 있지.
KBS, MBC, SBS방송국과 5대 신문사가 있어.
'자유로'를 달려가면 임진강 건너 세계 유일의
군사분계선(DMZ)과 북한이 보이지.

Contents of Hongdae Street

35 minutes from Incheon International Airport,
15 minutes from Gimpo International Airport,
If you ride the airport railroad, you will arrive at Hongik University Station.
It is where the airport railroad and subway line 2 reach.

Hongdae Street is full of Hallyu.
Music, food, movies, plays, fashion, cosmetics, medical care, jewelry, live performances,
Every corner of the alley is full of K-Culture.
It seems similar, but it's full of different flavors, styles, notes, and colors. And above all, a place full of passion for youth.

A place where young people from all over the world meet and interact a sacred place of culture where many different cultures come together and converge.
That's why Hallyu fans and fandom come from all over the world.

On the west side of Hongik University Street, the Han River flows across the Korean Peninsula,
Within a 20-kilometer radius, there are Gyeongbokgung Palace, Changgyeonggung Palace, Gwanghwamun, Namsan, Cheong Wa

Dae, President's Office, Seoul Station, and Itaewon International Street.

Yonsei University, Ewha Womans University, Sogang University, Chugae Art University, Gyeonggi University, and Dongguk University.

There are World Cup Stadium, Park, Sky Park, Dongdaemun Market, and Namdaemun Market.

There are KBS, MBC, and SBS stations and five major newspapers.

If you run along the Freeway, you will see the world's only Military Demarcation Line (DMZ) and North Korea across the Imjin River.

Korean Soldiers Patrolling the Southern Limit Line

사랑으로 충만한 거리

홍대거리는 한류 문화의 저수지야.
그곳에는 고향을 찾아오는 연어처럼
한류 문화를 찾는 사람들이 모여서 즐기지.
보고 듣고 배우고 느끼고 마시고 춤추고 대화하고,
아, 그리고 사랑을 나눌 수 있는 곳.
그곳은 21세기 세계 젊은이들의 문화 용광로,
세계 문화를 녹여 누구든 입맛에 맞게 조리해 주는 곳.

청춘의 본성은 움직이는 것,
젊음은 사랑과 정열을 발산하는 세대,
자유와 평등과 상호 존중이 숨 쉬는 존(Zone)이 필요해.
영어, 중국어, 불어, 독어, 아랍어, 일어, 스페인어, 베트남어,
태국어, 러시아어가 혼용되는 언어 천국인 홍대거리.
의사소통은 눈빛만으로도 가능하지.
홍대거리에 가면 따뜻한 음성이 우리를 반긴다.
'안녕하세요!'
'어서 오세요!'
'반갑습니다.'
'감사합니다.'라고-.

A street full of love

HongDae Street is a reservoir of Hallyu culture.
It's like salmon coming to hometown
People who are looking for Hallyu culture gather and enjoy it.
See, hear, learn, feel, drink, dance and talk,
Oh, and a place where we can make love.
It's a cultural melting pot for young people in the 21st century.
A place that melts world culture and cooks it to anyone's taste.

The nature of youth is to move,
Youth is a generation that radiates love and passion,
We need a zone where freedom, equality and mutual respect breathe.
Hongik University Street, a language paradise where English, Chinese, French, German, Arabic, Japanese, Spanish, Vietnamese, Thai, and Russian are mixed.
Communication is possible only with the eyes.
When we go to Hongdae Street, a warm voice welcomes us.
"Hello!"
"Welcome!"
"Nice to meet you."
"Thank you."

한류 문화의 지중해

세상은 문화 시대야, 문화적인 인간을 요구하고 있어.
천지인 삼위일체 사상, 홍익인간 정신이 가득한 인간,
그런 인종들을 등장시켜 평화 세계를 이끌려고 하는 거야.
그 일차 광장의 하나가 바로 홍대거리야.
홍대거리는 문화의 지중해요,
하나하나의 점포 스폿(spot)이 중세의 크레타섬이야.

홍대거리에 오면 누구나 선장, 조종사, 철학자, 예술인이야.
인생이라는 긴 항해를 준비하는 사람들,
자기의 소질을 펴고 싶은 사람들,
세상을 향해 제 주장을 알리고 싶은 사람들이
더불어 조용한 혁명을 위해 교류하고 수행하는 곳이지.
그들은 싸구려 장사꾼도 노랭이도 아니다.
제 일을 즐기는 사람들이야.
미래는 이런 사람들이 주인이 되지.

The Mediterranean Sea of Hallyu Culture

The modern world is a cultural age, it's asking for a cultural human being.
The idea of the Trinity of Heaven and Earth, a human being full of the human spirit of Hongik,
They are trying to lead a peaceful world by featuring such races.
One of the first squares is Hongdae Street.
HongaDae Street is underground of culture,
Each store spot is a medieval island of Crete.

If you come to Hongdae Street, everyone is a captain, pilot, philosopher, and artist.
People preparing for the long voyage of life,
People who want to show their talents,
People who want to make their point to the world
In addition, it is a place to exchange and carry out for a quiet revolution.
They are neither cheap traders nor tightwad.
They're the ones who enjoy their work.
In the future, these people become the owners.

큰 세상을 그리는 사람들

홍(弘)이란 '넓다(wide)'와 '널리(widely)'의 의미로서,
한국인의 심성을 한마디로 표현한 거야.
'넓다'는 크다, 길다, 너그럽다, 살갑다, 풍부하다.
'널리'는 광범하게, 너그럽게 베푼다는 의미.
대(大)는 크다는 뜻.
그래서 홍대는 넓고 크다는 '한(韓, Han)'의 세상을 말하지.
물론, 홍익대(弘益大)의 약칭이기도 해.

한국에 340여 개의 대학이 있고,
유명세를 타는 대학로(大學路)도 여럿 있지만,
서울 마포의 홍익대학교 앞이 한류의 대표 거리가 된 것은
무엇 때문일까?
홍(弘)이라는 명칭과 수천 년 이어온 삶의 철학 때문이야.
홍대거리는 한국인들의 삶의 축소판이야.

수백 년 전, 이곳은 배가 드나드는 포구였지.
고기잡이배들이 드나들던 곳이 마포(麻浦)였어.
삼(麻)을 재배하고 무역하던 작은 어촌이
지금은 글로벌 한류 문화의 포구가 되었지.
역시 홍(弘)이라는 문자는 넓고 깊고 위대해.

People who miss the big world

Hong(弘) means "wide" and "widely."
It's a word that expresses the heart of Koreans.
"Wide" is big, long, generous, tender, rich.
"Widely" means to give broadly and generously.
Dae(大) means large.
That's why Hongdae refers to the world of 'Han' that is wide and large.
Of course, it is also an abbreviation of Hongikdae(弘益大).

There are about 340 universities in Korea,
There are a number of famous university roads,
What made Hongik University in Mapo, Seoul become the representative street of the Korean Wave?
It's because of the name Hong(弘) and the philosophy of life that's been around for thousands of years.
HongDae Street is a microcosm of Korean life.

Hundreds of years ago, this was a port where ships came and went.
Mapo(麻浦) was the place where fishing boats came and went, a small fishing village that grew and traded flax.
It is now a port of global Korean Wave culture.
As expected, the character Hong(弘) is wide, deep, and great.

독도(獨島, Dokdo)
Dokdo is the easternmost island of Korean territory

3장

한류의 바탕은 옳은 정신
한국인에게는 정이라는 독특한 에너지가 있다
한국의 좋은 기후와 한류
한국은 세계 식물공원
한류는 다져진 문화
한류는 인류몽(人類夢)을 꿈꾼다
한류의 혼(魂 Spirit)
한류의 흥(興 Fun)
한류의 멋(態 Elegance)
한류의 맛(味 Taste)

한류의 바탕은 옳은 정신

한국인은 다양한 기후로 원만함과 인내심, 개척정신을 가졌지.
고난을 즐기며 힘을 모아 이겨내는 공동의 지혜를 터득한 거야.
많은 드라마에서 보았듯이 남자들의 헌신도 눈물겹고,
이웃과 어려운 사람을 돕는 두레, 향약(鄕約)을 발전시켰어.
모두의 행복을 만들어내는 공동체문화가 한류 문화의 뿌리야.

세계가 한국을 주목한 것은 20세기 후반이야.
전쟁의 상처를 국민이 단결하여 치유하고,
가난을 스스로 물리치고 일어서는 것을 보면서,
한국을 '희망을 주는 나라'로 인식하기 시작했지.
산업화에 이어 민주화가 이루어지는 굽힘 없는 민주주의의 여정,
500년 절대왕정에서 단번에 민주공화국으로 천지개벽한 변화와
놀라운 적응을 발휘하는 국민성.

올림픽과 월드컵을 개최하는 능력이 어디서 나왔을까?
공산권에 대한 개방의 자신감이 어디서 나왔을까?
세계가 한국을 주목하기 시작했어.
우린 고난은 사람과 사회를 강하게 만든다는 사실을 발견했지.
한국의 유구한 역사, 고유문화와 전통의 힘이 뒷받침되고,
공존과 상생의 지혜를 터득하고 살아왔기에 가능했어.
한류에서 먼저 배워야 할 것은 바로 이러한 정신과 의지야.

The Korean Wave is based on the right spirit

Koreans have a sense of smoothness, patience, and pioneering spirit with various climates.
They have learned the common wisdom of enjoying hardship and overcoming it by gathering strength.
As you've seen in many dramas, the dedication of men is also tearful.
We developed Dure, Hyangyak(鄕約), which helps neighbors and people in need.
Community culture that creates happiness for everyone is the root of Hallyu culture.

It was in the late 20th century that the world paid attention to Korea.
The wounds of war are healed by the unity of the people,
Watching them stand up against poverty by themselves,
Korea is starting to recognize it as an uplifting country.
The journey of unbending democracy followed by industrialization,
The national character that demonstrates a remarkable adaptation and a change from an absolute monarchy in 500 years to a democratic republic at once.

Where did the ability to host the Olympics and the World Cup come from?
Where did the confidence of opening up to the communist bloc come from?
The world is starting to pay attention to Korea.
We found that hardship makes people and society strong.
Korea's long history, unique culture, and traditional power are supported,
It was possible because They had learned the wisdom of coexistence and win-win relationship.
The first thing to learn from the Korean Wave is this spirit and will.

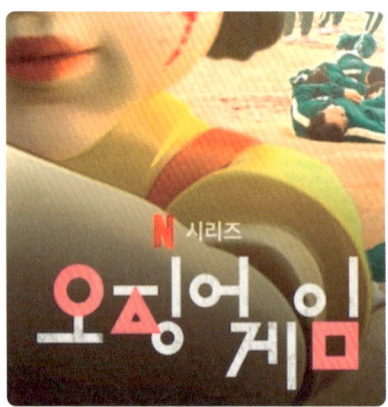

'Squid Game' is a Korean thriller survival drama series that aired on Netflix in 2021.

한국인에게는 정이라는 독특한 에너지가 있다

한국인들의 머리에는 인의예지(仁義禮智),
가슴에는 측은지심(惻隱之心)이 가득해.
그것들은 인류 공영과 발전을 도모하는 본원적인 철학이지.
그것이 실생활에서는 바로 정(情 affection)으로 표현돼.
정다운 사람, 정다운 이웃이 되려는 행동으로 나타나지.
세계 230개 민족 중에서 이런 깊고 따뜻한 휴머니즘을 지닌
민족은 드물 거야.

정이란 마음[心]에 푸름[靑]이 가득한 '하늘의 심성'을 말하지.
인간이 가져야 하는 원초적 본성인 인정을 말해.
비록 내 배가 고파도 콩 한 쪽도 갈라 나누는,
따뜻하고 푸근한 정으로 기대고 사는 마음을 말해.
어렵고 불쌍한 이웃에게 자기의 식품과 옷 그리고 돈과 피까지
나눠주는 사람들이 한국인이야.
한국의 역사는 정으로 이어온 진짜 인간의 역사야.
그래서 한국에는 '태초에 정이 있었다'고 말해.
그 정이 만들어 낸 것이 한류(韓流)라는 문화야.
한류를 이해하려면 한국인이 지닌 '정의 문화'를 알아야 해.

Koreans have a unique energy called affection

Korean people are generous, righteous, polite, and wise.
Their hearts are full of pity for the misfortune of others.
They are fundamental philosophies that promote human co-prosperity and development.
In real life, it is expressed as Jung(affection).
It appears as an act of being a friendly person, a friendly neighbor.
Of the 230 ethnic group in the world, few have such deep and warm humanism.

Jung(affection) refers to the 'heart of the sky' full of greenness in the heart.
It refers to recognition, which is the primary nature of human beings.
Even if I'm hungry, I'll split a slice of beans,
It's about how you lean on and live with warm and cozy feelings.
Koreans are the ones who give their food, clothes, money and blood to their neighbors who are in need.
Korea's history is a real human history that has led to love.
So in Korea, they say, 'In the beginning, there was affection.'
The culture of Hallyu(Korean Wave) was created by that affection.
To understand the Korean Wave, you need to know the 'affection culture' of Koreans.

한국의 좋은 기후와 한류

한국은 기후가 좋아서 살기 좋은 곳이지.
지구가 기후 재앙으로 요동치지만 그래도 한국은 딴 곳보단 나아.
4계절 따라 기후가 변하고, 모든 동식물이 특색있게 성장해.
그래서 한국의 음식 재료는 다른 나라와는 달라.
K-food가 발달한 이유가 바로 기후와 토양 때문이야.
같은 온대성 기후지대라도 한반도는 달라.
화산과 지진 등 큰 자연의 보복이 없는 온건한 땅이거든.
사람들도 기후를 닮아 역동적이지만 모질지 않아.

대륙성 기후와 해양성 기후를 동시에 지닌 독특한 기후.
봄 여름 가을 겨울이라는 역동적인 사계절이 존재하지.
봄은 동남풍이 불어 따뜻하고 비가 내려 대지를 깨우고,
여름은 북태평양 고기압의 영향으로 무덥고 장마가 지며,
가을은 오호츠크해의 이동성 고기압의 영향으로 맑고 건조하고,
겨울에는 한랭 건조한 시베리아 대륙성 고기압의 영향을 받아
춥고 건조하고, 눈이 많이 내리지.
그래서 모든 산업이 고루 발전하고 신기술이 발전해.
또 식물들이 모두 약성(藥性)을 띠고 있어서
한국의 식물성 식품 재료는 모두가 약효가 있어.

Korea's Good Climate and Hallyu

Korea has a nice climate, so it's a good place to live.
The earth fluctuates due to a climate disaster, but Korea is better than anywhere else.
The climate changes according to the four seasons, and all animals and plants grow characteristically. So Korean food ingredients are different from other countries.
The reason why K-food developed is because of the climate and soil. Even in the same temperate climate zone, the Korean Peninsula is different. It's a moderate land without major natural retaliation such as volcanoes and earthquakes. People are dynamic because they resemble the climate, but they are not vicious and fierce.

A unique climate with both continental and oceanic climates.
There are four dynamic seasons of spring, summer, autumn, and winter.
In spring, the southeastern wind blows and warms and rains to awaken the earth,
Summer is hot and rainy due to the influence of the North Pacific high pressure,
Autumn is clear and dry under the influence of mobile anticyclone in the Okhotsk Sea,

In winter, it is cold, dry, and snowy under the influence of cold, dry Siberian continental high pressure.

So all industries develop evenly and new technologies develop.

And plants are all medicinal

Plant-based food ingredients in Korea are all medicinal.

한국은 세계의 식물공원

한국 땅에 자라는 식물 수는 5,000여 종,
이 숫자는 유럽 전체를 합친 것보다 많아.
그래, 한국은 '전 세계 식물백화점'이지.
그중 2,600종은 식용이고, 또 그중 1,200종은 약초야.
한국의 산야에서 자라는 식물은 독초만 빼곤 모두 음식 재료야.
자연인들은 산에서 나는 식품 재료만으로 살아갈 수가 있어.

같은 소나무라도 툰드라지대의 소나무는 목재와 땔감일 뿐,
그러나 한국의 소나무는 약재로도 쓰여.
한국 땅에서 나는 다양한 쑥은 모두가 식용 또는 약초야.
그래서 단군신화(檀君神話) 같은 스토리가 생긴 거지
마늘과 쑥을 먹고 곰이 여자가 됐다는 신화 말야.

그게 사실일까?
아니지, 이 땅의 쑥과 마늘이 약효가 풍부한 약재였다는 말이지.
외국의 쑥은 독성이 있어서 못 먹는 그냥 잡풀일 뿐이야.
한국의 쑥은 온갖 음식을 만드는 천연 식품 재료야.
한국의 약초를 외국에 옮겨 심으면 쓸모없는 들풀로 변하고,
한국의 인삼을 외국에 가져가 키우면, 약효가 확 낮아진대.
모두가 기후와 토양의 영향 때문이지.
4계절 기후변화가 모든 식물에게 속 깊은 성질을 갖게 한 거지.

Korea is the world's botanical park

The number of plants growing on Korean soil is about 5,000.
This number is more than all of Europe combined.
Yes, Korea is a 'plant department store all over the world.'
2,600 of them are edible, and 1,200 of them are medicinal herbs.
Plants that grow in mountains and fields in Korea are all food ingredients except for poisonous plants.
Natural people can only survive on food ingredients from the mountains.

Even if it's the same pine tree, the pine tree in the tundra is just wood and firewood.
But Korean pine trees are also used as medicinal ingredients.
Various mugwort from Korean soil are all edible or herbal.
That's why it's like the myth of Dangun(檀君神話)
The myth that a bear became a woman after eating garlic and mugwort.

Is that true?
No, mugwort and garlic in this land were medicinal herbs.
Foreign mugwort is just a weed that you can't eat because it's toxic.
Korean mugwort is a natural food ingredient that makes all kinds

of food.

If you plant Korean herbs abroad, they turn into useless grasses,

If you take Korean ginseng abroad and raise it, the effectiveness of the medicine will decrease significantly.

It's all because of the effects of climate and soil.

Climate change in four seasons has given all plants a deep nature.

Tourists on the streets of Hongik University

한류는 오랜 역사의 산물

한류(Korea Wave)는 한때의 유행이 아냐.
심오한 정신, 긴 역사의 뿌리가 만든, 도도하고 단단한 문명이야.
'널리 인간 세상을 이롭게 하자'는 홍익인간의 한국 정신은
5억 년의 역사가 살아 숨 쉬는 한국 산하의 산물이야.
이 땅에는 70만 년 전에 구석기인들이 살았지.
그들은 고아시아인, 아이누인들이었어.
그들은 빙하기에 다 사멸하여 사라졌지만,
석회동굴에 숨어 빙하기를 이겨내고 살아남은 사람들이
제3 빙하기가 지나자 동굴에서 나와 신석기 문명을 만들었어.
수많은 조개 무덤이 그것을 증명하지.

그들이 한반도와 만주를 거점으로 역사를 꾸렸어.
북방대륙에서 내려온 사람들과
남방에서 올라온 해양족들도 여기에 가세하여
그들은 토착인들과 힘을 합해 독특한 문명을 만들었어.
현대 한국인과 DNA가 많이 닮은 종족은 부랴트족, 몽골족,
라후족, 만주족이야. 그들은 한민족과 조상이 같거든.
한반도 땅은 구석기 문명부터 살아있는 박물관이야.
국토 어디든지 문화유물 유적이 가득해.

The Korean Wave is a product of a long history

The Korean Wave is not the one-time trend.
It's a proud, solid civilization created by a profound spirit, a long history of roots.
Hongik's Korean spirit of "Let's benefit the human world."
It's a product of Korea's 500 million years of history.
This land was inhabited by Paleolithic people 700,000 years ago.
They were the ancient Asian people, Ainu.
They all died and disappeared during the Ice Age.
People who survived the ice age by hiding in limestone caves
After the Third Ice Age, they came out of the cave and created a Neolithic civilization. Countless seashell tombs prove it.

They made history based on the Korean Peninsula and Manchuria.
The people who came down from the northern continent
The ocean people from the south also joined this
They joined forces with indigenous people to create a unique civilization.

The ethnic groups that have a lot of DNA similar to modern Koreans are the Buryat, Mongol, Rahu, and Manchu. They are the same ancestor as the Korean people.

The land of the Korean peninsula is a living museum from the Old Stone Age civilization.
Everywhere in the country is full of cultural relics.

영화 '기생충'
In the Korean movie 'Parasite'

한류는 인류몽(人類夢)을 꿈꾼다

한류의 목표는 인류몽(the dream of mankind)이야.
80억 인류가 함께 평화와 번영을 누리자는 꿈.
그것이 바로 한국인들이 꿈꾸는 홍익인간 정신이지.
모든 생명체와 무생물까지 인간으로 인정하고, 존중하고
보호하지.
한국인들은 그래야 진짜 인류 평화와 행복이 온다고 믿고 있어.
한류는 마음에서 마음으로 전해지는 정신요소가 버무려진 것이야.
그것들이 역사와 문화 속에서 일어나고 성장해서 한국인의
성격과 문화의 특성으로 발전한 거야.
그리고 창조적 DNA가 그때그때 나타나서 합해졌지.

한국인은 '한국몽'이 아니라 '인류몽'을 갖고 살았어.
그래서 그들은 평화국가, 평화국민이라는 자부심이 있어.
그들은 앉아서 기다리는 평화론자가 아니라, 세계 각지에
찾아가서 도움을 주는 적극적인 평화실천가들이야.
즉 경제협력, 교육과 문화예술, 스포츠나 의료봉사, 재난구호,
난민구호를 위해 찾아가지.
한류가 세계로 전파되는 것도 널리 인간세계를 이롭게 하는 실천이야.
BTS 보컬의 정신과 활동 역시 홍익인간에 부합하는 거야.
BTS의 꿈은 '인류몽'에 있어.

The Korean Wave Dreams of Humanity

The goal of Hallyu is the dream of the mankind.
The dream of 8 billion human beings enjoying peace and prosperity together.
That's the Hongik human spirit that Koreans dream of.
Recognize, respect, and protect all living and inanimate objects as human beings. They believe that only then will real human peace and happiness come.
Hallyu is a combination of mental elements that are conveyed from the heart to the heart.
They happen and grow in history and culture and develop into Korean characteristics and cultural characteristics.
And then the creative DNA came along and put together.

Koreans lived with 'human dreams', not 'Korean dreams.'
So they are proud to be a peaceful nation, a peaceful people.
They are not pacifists who sit down and wait, but active peace practitioners who visit and help around the world.
In other words, they go to economic cooperation, education and culture and arts, sports and medical services, disaster relief and refugee relief.
The spread of the Korean Wave to the world is also a practice that benefits the human world widely.
The spirit and activities of the BTS vocals are also in line with the Hongik people.
BTS' dream is to be 'Human Dream.'

한류의 혼(魂 Spirit)

한국인은 세상을 바른 이치로 대하고,
개인이 주위 사람들과 사물에 생기(vitality)를 주고
삶의 의욕을 갖도록 추동하는 철학을 지니고 살지.
이러한 홍익인간 정신이 한국 역사와 문화의 바탕을 이루었어.

한민족은 하늘과 땅(자연)과 사람을 하나로 봐.
그로 인해 독특한 천제(天祭) 문화가 생겼어.
그들은 하늘과 땅과 조상에 성대하게 제사를 드리지.
한민족은 하늘을 공경하고, 조상을 숭배하는 사상을 소중히 해.
국교(國敎)는 없고, 하늘, 땅, 사람 존중을 실천하지.
세계 어느 종교든 인정하고 존중하는 나라야.
대한민국에 해를 끼치지 않는다면 어느 종교도 자유야.
한국에는 종교 간에 전쟁이나 대립 갈등, 다툼이 없어.
각 민족이나 개인의 혼과 얼을 존중하기 때문이지.
앞으로 종교 유엔을 만든다면 한국이 최적지일 거야.

Spirit of the Korean Wave

Koreans treat the world in the right way,
The individual gives vitality to the people and things around him
Live with a philosophy that drives others to live.
This Hongik human spirit formed the basis of Korean history and culture.

The Korean people see heaven and earth(nature) and people as one.
It created a unique heavenly culture.
They offer grand memorial services to heaven and earth and to their ancestors.
The Korean people cherish the idea of honoring the sky and worshipping ancestors.
There is no national religion, and they practice respect for heaven, earth, and people.
It is a country that recognizes and respects any religion in the world.
Any religion is free as long as it doesn't harm the Republic of Korea.
In Korea, there is no war, conflict, or quarrel between religions.
It's because it respects the soul and soul of each ethnic group or individual.
If we make a religious UN in the future, Korea will be the best place.

한류의 흥(興 Fun)

흥은 한국인이 지닌 정서의 핵(核)이야.
흥을 신명(神明)이나 신바람이라고도 하지.
한국인은 '파이팅!'을 잘 외치지.
그것은 신명을 내자는 뜻이야.
사람의 능력을 초월하는 기운이 뻗치게 하자는 말이지.
사람에게도 신성(神性)이 있다고 믿고 있으니까.

신명을 지피는 방법 중에 노래와 춤이 있지.
한국인은 모두가 가수요 춤꾼이라고 보면 돼.
누구나 노래하고 막춤과 탈춤을 추지.
싸이의 말춤은 가장 보편적인 한국인의 막춤이야.
힘든 일을 할 때도 노동요(勞動謠)라는 노래와 춤이 있어.

신명나는 흥이 곧 K팝, 노래방문화, 노래자랑이지.
사물놀이와 판소리도 신명을 지피는 율동이야.
한국에는 독특한 흥타령 문화인 민속놀이가 많아.
그것은 사당패놀이, 광대놀이, 차전놀이, 기마전, 줄다리기,
제기차기, 윷놀이, 자치기, 연날리기, 팽이치기 같은 것.
이런 놀이가 영화와 드라마의 콘텐츠가 되었지.
또 발달한 정보기술과 만나 인터넷 게임을 만들었어.
한국이 게임 강국이 된 것은 결코 우연이 아니야.

The Fun of the Korean Wave

Heung(興) is the core of Korean emotion.
It is also called 'Shinmyeong' or 'Shinbaram.'
Koreans often shout fighting! It means to live a new life.
I'm saying let's give it a boost that's beyond human capacity.
They believe that people have divinity.

Singing and dancing are some of the ways to live a new life.
All Koreans are singers and dancers.
Everyone sings and dances and mask dances.
Psy's horse-riding dance is the most common Korean dance.
Even in the workplace, they do hard work and sing and dance.

The exciting excitement is K-pop, karaoke culture, and singing.
Samulnori and pansori are also dances that make people happy.
There are many folk games in Korea, which is a unique Heungtaryeong culture.
It is a game of sadangpae, a game of clowns, a game of chariots, a game of horseback, a tug of war, Jegichagi, Yutnori, Jachigi, kite flying, a spinning top, etc.
This kind of play became the content of movies and dramas.
They also met with advanced information technology and made an internet game. It is no coincidence that Korea has become an game powerful nation.

한류의 멋(態 Elegance)

한국인의 멋은 K-fashion, K-beauty에 있어.
한복은 세계가 알아주는 고상하고 아름다운 옷.
현대 옷도 디자인과 색감이 뛰어나 세계 패션계에 영향력이 크지.
뛰어난 패션 감각이 옷 산업과 염색 산업을 키웠고,
화장품과 헤어스타일, 가발, 성형 의술, 보석에까지 이르게 됐어.
영화와 연극, 회화, 조각, 웹툰, 캘리그라피 등으로도 나타나지.
특히 한국 화장품은 인삼, 개펄의 진흙(mud)까지 이용하여
독자적인 크림을 만들었어.
외국 관광객들은 한국 화장품을 최애(最愛) 상품으로 인정하지.

한국의 멋은 한글(Hangeul)에도 나타나 있어.
자음 14자, 모음 10자,
총 24자로 이루어진 한글은,
상형성(象形性)이 아름답고 뛰어나서
패션 문자로 자리 잡아,
각종 옷이나 장신구에 새기고 있어.

The beauty of the Korean Wave (Elegance)

Korean fashion is in K-fashion, K-beauty.
Hanbok is a noble and beautiful dress that the world recognizes.
Modern clothes are also very influential in the world's fashion world because of their design and color.
A great sense of fashion nurtured the clothing and dyeing industries,
Cosmetics, hairstyle, wigs, plastic surgery, jewelry.
It also appears in movies, plays, paintings, sculptures, webtoons, and calligraphy.
In particular, Korean cosmetics made their own creams using ginseng and mud of mudflats.
Foreign tourists recognize Korean cosmetics as their favorite product.

The beauty of Korea is also shown in Hangeul.
Hangeul consists of 14 consonants, 10 vowels, 24 characters in total,
It is beautiful and excellent, and it becomes a fashion character.
They're engraving it on all kinds of clothes and jewelry.

한류의 맛(味 Taste)

K-food의 특징은 천인상응(天人相應)이야.
자연과 인간이 하나 되어 어울리는 맛이지.
조미료조차도 천연의 식재료를 사용하니까.
김치, 떡볶이, 치맥, 김치전, 파전, 녹두전은 세계 음식이 됐어.
김치는 유네스코에 등재된 세계 5대 발효식품이지.
한국 고추장은 맵지만 달아.
된장, 간장, 고추장은 모두 콩과 천일염으로 만든 것이야.
이 3대 장(醬)이 한국 음식의 맛을 내는 기본이지.

한국의 떡은 서양의 케이크나 빵보다 맛난 음식이야.
찰떡, 시루떡, 절편, 감자떡, 쑥떡, 인절미, 팥떡, 수수떡,
망개떡, 보리개떡, 구름떡, 무지개떡이 있어.
요즘은 서양의 케이크를 쌀로 만든 쌀케이크도 나왔어.

또한 불고기, 돼지족발, 국밥, 두루치기, 김밥, 순대, 잡채,
삼계탕, 꼬리곰탕, 비빔밥, 치킨, 냉면, 라면도 상위그룹이지.
비빔밥은 다양한 종류의 음식을 한 번에 섞어 먹는 영양식.
라면은 매월 1억 달러 이상 수출되는 세계인의 음식이지.
최근 개발된 '불닭볶음면'은 일 년에 9억 개씩 수출한대.
그리고 치맥(치킨+맥주)도 세계인이 좋아하지.
막걸리, 백세주, 인삼주, 머루 포도주 등 술도 빼놓을 수 없어.

Taste of Korean wave

The characteristic of K-food is that nature and humans communicate with each other.
It's a taste that combines nature and humans.
Even condiments use natural ingredients.
Kimchi, tteokbokki, chicken and beer, kimchi pancake, green onion pancake, and mung bean pancake became world food.
Kimchi is one of the world's top five fermented foods listed on UNESCO.
Korean gochujang is spicy but sweet.
Soybean paste, soy sauce, and red pepper paste are all made from beans and sea salt.
These three pastes are the basis for the taste of Korean food.

Korean rice cakes are more delicious than Western cakes and breads.
There are rice cakes, Sirutteok, Jeolpyeon, potato rice cakes, mugwort rice cakes, injeolmi, red bean rice cakes, sorghum rice cakes, manggae rice cakes, barley rice cakes, cloud rice cakes.
These days, there is also a cake made of rice from Western cakes.

Bulgogi, Pork Jokbal, Rice Soup, Duruchigi, Kimbap, Sundae, Japchae, Samgyetang, Tail Gomtang, Bibimbap, Chicken, Cold

Noodles, and Ramen are also in the top groups.

Bibimbap is a nutritional food that mixes various kinds of food at once.

Ramen is a food from people around the world that is exported more than 100 million dollars a month.

The recently developed 'Buldak Stir-fried Noodles' exports 900 million units a year.

And chicken and beer (chimaek) is also loved by people around the world.

Alcohol such as makgeolli, baekseju, ginseng wine, and muru wine are also indispensable.

a delicious bowl of bulgogi

백두산 천지(높이 2750m)가 구름에 덮혀있다.
Baekdusan Mountain's Cheonji (2,750 meters high) is covered by clouds.

4장

장(醬)의 노래

한류와 유목주의(Nomadism)

자연 친화적인 삶

백남준(白南準)을 아시나요?

한류 3.0시대

한국인의 신심(信心)

한류는 신인류가 완성한다

한류 문명의 사명

장(醬)의 노래

한국 음식은 장(醬)으로 시작되지.
간장 된장 고추장 막장 쌈장 청국장 등이야.
콩을 삶아 다져서 메주를 만들고,
짚으로 묶어 햇빛과 바람에 숙성시키지.
큰 독 안에 천연소금물을 부어 메주를 띄워 익히면 돼.
장은 하늘과 땅과 우주가 인정하는 음식이야.

장은 사람의 건강을 구하는 천연식품,
그것으로 빚어낸 한류 식품 문명이 인류의 식탁을 열지.
장은 하늘과 땅의 기운을 사람이 받아,
정성으로 만든 우주식품이야.

Meju, made by boiling beans, is the
basis of Korean food.

Songs by Jang(醬)

Korean food starts with paste.
They are soy sauce, soybean paste, red pepper paste, marinated sauce, and cheonggukjang.
Boil and mince beans to make fermented soybeans,
Tie it with straw and age it in the sun and wind.
Pour natural salt water into a large jar and cook it with fermented soybean lump.
Jang is a food recognized by heaven, earth, and space.

Jang is a natural food that saves people's health,
The Korean Wave food civilization created by it opens the table for mankind.
The Jang receives the energy of heaven and earth,
It's a space food made with sincerity.

한류와 유목주의(Nomadism)

한국은 부지런하고 활기찬 아침의 나라야.
조용히 흐르는 물 아래에는 엄청난 에너지가 있지.
한국인의 국민성은 침착, 근면, 성실, 인내, 염치야.
한국인은 역동적이고 개척심, 모험심이 강해.

세계 220개 국가에 K팝과 K드라마를 전파한 것은
유목민다운 가치관과 역동성, 추진력이 있어서 가능했지.
좁은 영토, 부족한 자원 국가인 한국이 살길은 개척, 모험이었어.
'하면 된다', '잘살아보세'라는 모토로 살아온 사람들,
한국인의 핏속에는 유목주의(Nomadism)가 흐르고 있어.
그들의 땀과 눈물 덕에 세계가 칭찬하는 나라가 됐지.
세계 젊은이들의 놀이문화에 K팝이 빠지지 않고 있잖아?

한류는 K팝에서 벗어나 풍부한 K-culture 시대를 열었지.
음악, 드라마, 영화와 연극, 연예, 웹툰, 음식, 패션, 쥬얼리,
주택. 교육과 의료, 건강산업, 한국어, 스포츠, 화장품을 비롯한
뷰티산업 등으로 확산하였지.
음악도 K팝 이외에 K-trot, 판소리도 한 영역을 차지하게 되었어.
이제 K-culture는 21세기 인류 신문명의 한 분야를 차지했어.

Hallyu and Nomadism

Korea is a country of diligent and lively mornings.
There's a lot of energy underneath the quietly flowing water.
The national character of Koreans is calm, hard work, sincerity, patience, and shame.
Koreans are dynamic, pioneering, and adventurous.

The spread of K-pop and K-drama to 220 countries around the world
It was possible because of its nomadic values, dynamism, and drive.
The way for Korea, a small territory and a scarce resource country, to live was pioneering and adventure.
Those who have lived under the motto of "You can do it" and "Live wel."
Nomadism is flowing in the blood of Koreans.
Thanks to their sweat and tears, the world has become a country that praises.
K-pop is not missing in the play culture of young people around the world, right?

The Korean Wave broke away from K-pop and ushered in an era of rich K-culture.
Music, drama, film and theater, entertainment, webtoons, food,

fashion, jewelry, housing.
It has spread to education, medical care, health industry, Korean language, sports, cosmetics, and beauty industry.
In addition to K-pop, K-trot and Pansori came to occupy an area.
Now K-culture is a field of 21st century human new civilization.

Hongik University Street is full of Korean Wave culture

한국인의 자연 친화적인 삶

어디에 사찰음식이 있더냐.
어디에 숯불갈비가 있더냐.
어디에 천연 염색이 있더냐.
어디에 온돌아파트가 있더냐.
어디에 한옥(韓屋)마을이 있더냐.
어디에 옻칠 자개장이 있더냐.
어디에 찜질방, 황토방이 있더냐.

아, 한국은 제2의 르네상스가 시작된 나라.
21세기 자연 친화의 신문명을 여는 나라.

자연의 기품과 혼을 생활 속에 끌어들여,
자연과 인간이 하나 되어 누리며 사는 나라.

Jjimjilbang is a personal healing method using heat

The nature-friendly lives of Koreans

Where is the temple food.
Where is charcoal-grilled ribs.
Where is the natural dyeing.
Where is the ondol apartment.
Where is the Hanok Village.
Where is the lacquered mother-of-pearl.
Where are jjimjilbangs and red clay room.

Oh, Korea is the country where the Second Renaissance began.
A country that opens up a new, nature-friendly civilization in the 21st century.

Bringing nature's dignity and soul into life,
a country where nature and humans live together as one.

백남준(白南準)을 아시나요?

세계 비디오아트의 창시자 백남준은 한류의 선각자야.
87년의 설치작품 <로봇-라디오맨>은
친구 요세르 보이즈의 죽음을 애도하는 애도 탑이었대.
1988년에 만든 <다다익선(多多益善)>은 1,003대의 TV로
만든 작품이지.
TV 브라운관 1,003대를 '피사의 사탑'처럼 쌓아 올려 영상을
띄워서 작가의 의도를 전달한 작품이야.
그 안의 영상 콘텐츠는 아름다운 한국의 산하, 집과 건축물,
탑과 왕릉, 고대 유물, 고구려 고분 벽화, 한국의 옷, 음식,
놀이와 춤 등이었어.
왜 TV 브라운관이 1,003대였을까?
그것은 10월 3일 개천절(開天節),
한국의 고대국가인 단군조선의
개국일을 나타내는 상징이었어.

한국인 백남준의 비디오아트는 가장
한국적인 콘텐츠를 담았고,
인류사에 제2의 르네상스를 연
시작이야.
백남준이 활동하던 70, 80년대는
한류의 창업(創業)기였어.

백남준 작품 <다다익선>
Paik Nam-june's work,
<Dadaikseon>

Do you know Paik Nam-june?

Nam June Paik, the founder of world video art, is a visionary of the Korean Wave.
"Robot-Radio Man" is an installation from '87
It was a mourning tower mourning the loss of his friend Yoser Boys.
Created in 1988, "Dadaiksun(the more the better)" is a production of 1,003 television sets.
It is a work that conveys the artist's intention by stacking 1,003 TV CRTs like the Leaning Tower of Pisa.
The video content inside was beautiful Korean mountains, houses and structures, towers and royal tombs, ancient relics, murals of Goguryeo tombs, Korean clothes, food, play, and dance.
Why were there 1,003 TV CRTs?
October 3rd is the day of the establishment of the country
It was a symbol of the founding of Dangun Joseon, an ancient country in Korea.

Korean Nam June Paik's video art contains the most Korean content,
It's the beginning of a second renaissance in human history.
In the '70s and '80s, when Paik was active, it was the start-up period of the Korean Wave Industry.

한류 3.0시대

90년대와 2000년대 초반은 한류의 개척기로
많은 실험이 세계 도처에서 나타났어.
앞으로 한류 3.0은 더 정교해지고 고급화할 거야.

그 방향은 좀 더 현실적이고 미래적이야.
한국의 '국가발전 학습(national learning)'의 성공 스토리 같은 것,
K팝을 넘어서 한국이 발전시킨 모든 것을 수출하게 되지.
그게 뭐냐구?
6차에 걸쳐 성공한 경제개발 5개년 계획(30년),
아름다운 도시계획과 발전책, 도시와 농어촌의 공존,
다문화가족의 성공, 세계 최대의 갯벌과 람사르 습지,
세계 제1의 허브 인천공항과 원자력 발전 기술,
해저터널과 긴 교량 건설기술,
사막에 농사짓는 법, 자동차와 조선업의 기적적인 발전,
병원과 의료체계, 행정, 교육, 방위산업,
새마을운동 등 한국이 개발한 신문명을 더 널리 알리게 돼.
문화예술의 소프트 콘텐츠는 말할 필요도 없지.
진정한 세계평화와 공동번영을 향해 나갈 거야.

The Korean Wave 3.0 era

The 90s and early 2000s were the pioneers of the Korean Wave.
A lot of experiments have appeared all over the world.
In the future, Hallyu 3.0 will become more sophisticated and advanced.

The direction is more realistic and futuristic.
Like the success story of Korea's 'national learning',
It will export everything that Korea has developed beyond K-pop.

What's that?
The five-year economic development plan(30 years) that was successful over six rounds,
Beautiful urban planning and development measures, coexistence of urban and rural areas,
The success of multicultural families, the world's largest mudflats and Namsar wetlands,
Incheon Airport, the world's No. 1 hub, and nuclear power generation technology, construction technology for undersea tunnels and long bridges,

How to farm in the desert, the miraculous development of automobiles and shipbuilding,

hospitals and healthcare systems, administration, education, defense,
New civilizations developed by Korea, such as Saemaul Undong, will be more widely known.
It goes without saying the soft content of culture and art.
We're going for real world peace and co-prosperity.

In front of AK Plaza full of tourists

한국인의 신심(信心)

한국의 전통 종교는 천신교(天神敎)야.
한국인은 예로부터 천신(하느님)을 섬긴 민족이야.
하늘을 두려워하고 공경하는 민족이라서,
하느님의 뜻에 거역하면 천벌 받는다고 믿었지.

한국의 불교사찰 뒤쪽에 있는 삼성각에 가보면,
칠성신, 산신, 독성신 등 삼성을 모시고 있어.
하늘과 땅, 인간을 소중히 하고, 무병장수와 평화, 풍년을
기원하는 한국인들.
그 제사를 주관하는 제주(祭主)를 천군(天君)이라 했어.
고조선의 첫 왕인 단군왕검도 천군이시지.
지금은 지방의 어른들이 천군이시고.

천신교의 경전은 <천부경(天符經)>이었어.
인간 삶의 기준을 81자로 정리한 경전이야.
기독교의 성경, 불교의 불경, 이슬람교의 코란과 같은 것이지.
한국인의 신심이 한류 문화의 콘텐츠를 만드는데 기여했어.

The devotion of the Korean people

The traditional religion in Korea is the heavenly religion.
Koreans are a people who have served God since ancient times.
We are a people who fear and respect heaven,
We believed that going against God's will would be punished by heaven.

If you go to Samseonggak in the back of a Buddhist temple in Korea, There are Samsung god, including the Chilseong god, the mountain god, and the great human god.
Koreans who cherish heaven, earth, and humans, and wish for good health, peace, and a good harvest.
The priest in charge of the ritual was called the king of heaven.
Dangun, the first king of Gojoseon, was a king from heaven.

Samseonggak, a traditional Korean religion in a Korean Buddhist temple.

Now, the adults in the provinces are the heavenly soldiers.

Heavenly religion has scriptures given by heaven.
It is a scripture that summarizes the standards of human life in 81 characters.
It's like the Bible of Christianity, the Buddhist scriptures, the Quran of Islam.
Korean faith has contributed to the creation of Hallyu culture's contents.

天符經

一始無始一析三極無
盡本天一一地一二人
一三一積十鉅無匱化
三天二三地二三人二
三大三合六生七八九
運三四成環五七一妙
衍萬往萬來用變不動
本本心本太陽昂明人
中天地一一終無終一

Cheon-bu-gyeong is the scriptures of the
Korean people from ancient times

한류는 신인류가 완성한다

인류 역사는 거대한 흐름이었다.
세기(世紀)가 바뀔 때마다 물결친 패러다임의 파도는
세상과 사람을 바꾸었지.
중세의 르네상스가 그랬듯이.
지금은 하늘의 섭리가 새로운 한류 문명을 소환하여
인류의 타락을 막는 구원의 소임을 맡긴 것이야.

한류 문화의 꿈은 정신과 물질의 균형 잡힌 발전,
인간과 자연이 하나 되어 겸양할 줄 아는 세상,
고난 속에서도 즐거움과 기쁨을 찾아내는 혜안(慧眼),
차별 없는 세상을 구현하라는 하느님의 명령을 이행하는 것이야.

작은 것에서 행복을 발견하고,
적은 것에서 만족을 누릴 줄 아는 신인류의 부활을 위해
뜻과 힘을 모으는 것이 한류 문명이고 한류인이야.

The Korean Wave is completed by the new human race

Human history has been a huge trend.
The paradigm wave that rippled every time the century changed.
It changed the world and the people.
Just like the Renaissance of the Middle Ages.
Now, the providence of the heaven has summoned a new Korean culture
It was entrusted to the task of saving humanity from corruption.

The dream of Hallyu culture is the balanced development of spirit and material,
A world where humans and nature can be united and humble,
Wisdom eyes that find joy and pleasure in the face of hardship,
To fulfill God's orders to realize a world free of discrimination.

Find happiness in small things,
For the resurrection of a new human being who can enjoy satisfaction from the small.
It is the Korean Wave civilization and the Korean Wave that brings together the will and power.

한류 문명의 사명

19세기 이후 200년간 산업화, 민주화가 발달하고,
과학과 물질문명이 고도로 발달했지만,
인간의 불행과 고통은 해결되지 않았어.
자유민주주의 자본주의가 희구하던 공영의 가치가
사악한 욕심의 구렁텅이로 빠져 불평등과 소외가 깊어졌고,
전체주의 공산주의가 등장하여 전쟁을 불러왔지.
50년대부터 30년간 냉전 시대가 지속되었어.
다행히 공산주의가 몰락하였고,
세계는 개혁 개방으로 30년 동안 평화를 누렸지.

그런데 지금도 지구에서 1분에 6명이 굶주려 죽어가고 있고,
공산 전체주의가 부활하여 유럽과 중동, 동북아에 위기를
불러와, 열전과 냉전이 범벅이 된 상황이 되고 말았어.
이것을 바로잡을 문명의 대전환이 필요한 시점이야.
세계 유일의 분단국이면서 성공한 국가,
한국에게 그 불을 끄라는 소명이 주어졌다고 생각해.
홍익인간 정신으로 세계인을 일깨워주고,
한류 문명을 인류 상생과 화합의 문명으로 등장시킨 거지.
이것은 인류 역사 발전의 필연이야.
세계인이 진정한 자유인, 한류인이 되는 날이 와야 해.

Mission of Korean Wave Civilization

In the 200 years since the 19th century, industrialization and democratization have developed,
Although science and material civilization are highly developed,
Human misfortune and suffering have not been resolved.
The value of public life that liberal democratic capitalism wanted
Inequality and alienation deepened after falling into the pit of evil greed,
Totalitarian communism came along and brought about war.
The Cold War lasted 30 years from the fifties.
Fortunately, communism fell,
The world enjoyed 30 years of peace with reform and openness.

But there are still six people on Earth who are starving to death in a minute,
Communist totalitarianism was revived, bringing crises to Europe, the Middle East, and Northeast Asia, and becoming a Hot War and Cold War.
It's time for a major civilization transformation to correct this.
The world's only divided nation and successful nation,
I think Korea has been given the call to put out the fire.
It awakens people around the world with a Hongik human spirit,
The Korean Wave civilization emerged as a civilization of

coexistence and harmony among mankind.

This is the inevitable development of human history.

The day should come when people from all over the world become truly free people and Hallyu people.

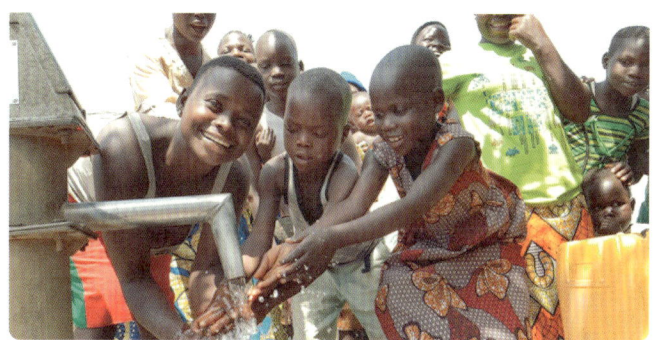

South Korean aid agency digs wells in Africa

세종(世宗, Sejong the Great)
한글을 제정하여 문예부흥을 주도한 조선의 세종대왕
King Sejong of Joseon led the revival of literature by enacting Hangeul

5장

한국은 어떤 나라인가?

불행을 극복한 한국인

한국은 부지런한 아침의 나라

한국의 성공 배경

한국 현대사의 두 위대한 지도자

한글(韓㐎, Hangeul) 찬가

한글은 한국 최고의 발명품

K-콘텐츠의 확대

한국은 어떤 나라인가?

영토는 10만㎢, 인구는 5,000만 명이지만
그들의 마음은 넓고 자유분방하지.
그들은 '널리 인간 세계를 이롭게 한다'는
글로벌 이익 사상을 갖고 살아.
한국인은 온 인류가 함께 잘 살기를 원해.
그래서 개도국이나 가난한 나라에 원조하고 있어.

한국은 70년 전에는 세계에서 가장 가난한 나라여서,
유엔 등 외국의 원조를 받고 살았어.
하지만 세계2차대전 후 독립한 102개 나라 중에서
이제는 개발도상국을 원조해주는 유일한 나라가 되었어.

70년간 휴전상태인 한국이
세계 국가로 도약한 비결을 찾아 긴 행렬이 이어진다.
세계 각국에서 인종과 종교,
나이와 성별을 초월하고 달려오는 사람들,
오늘도 한국 땅에는 백만 명의 한류 팬이 붐빈다.
전통문화와 현대문화가 조화로운 곳곳마다.

Korea, what kind of country?

It has a territory of 100,000 square kilometers and a population of 50 million
Their hearts are wide and free-spirited.
They live with the idea of global interest, 'benefiting the wide human world.'
Koreans want the whole human race to live well together.
So they are giving aid to developing countries or poor countries.

Korea was the poorest country in the world 70 years ago,
They lived with foreign aid such as the United Nations.
But out of 102 countries that gained independence after World War ll
Now it's the only country that provides aid to others.

South Korea, which has been in a truce for 70 years
A long procession continues in search of the secret to becoming a world country.
People who come from all over the world, regardless of race, religion, age, and gender,
There are still a million Korean Wave fans in Korea today.
Everywhere traditional and modern culture harmonizes.

불행을 극복한 한국인

한국은 역사상 941회의 외세의 침략을 받았지만
한 번도 남을 침략하지 않은 평화국가였어.
예절 바른 선비의 나라,
정의롭고 정직하고 개척적인 민주국가이지.

한국인의 따뜻하고 성실한 인심을 만나보고,
진정한 자아 발견과 세계사의 신 흐름을 흡입하고,
미래를 여는 에너지를 얻고자 찾아오는 사람들이
한 해에 2천만 명이야.

한국에서 배우는 것은 기술, 새마을운동뿐이 아니다.
지극히 인간적인 문화의 힘과 열정,
우리는 불과 30년 만에 빈국에서 선진국이 된
국가 경영의 비법을 탐색하지.
앞으로는 문화가 경쟁력이 되는 시대라서
한류 문명의 가치가 전통적인 제조업을 훨씬 능가하게 되거든.
한류 시장은 2024년도에 760억 달러(한화 100조 원)이고
2030년에는 1,430억 달러(한화 190조 원)로 예상하고 있어.

Koreans Overcome Misfortunes

Korea has been invaded 941 times in history by foreign powers.
But it was a peaceful country that never invaded others.
A nation of well-mannered scholars,
It's a just, honest, pioneering democracy.

Meet the warm and sincere heart of the Korean people,
It breathes in real self-discovery and the new flow of world history.
The people who come to get the energy to open the future
It's 20 million a year.

It is not just technology and Saemaul Undong that they learn in Korea.
The power and passion of a very human culture,
We explore the secrets of national management from poor to advanced countries in just 30 years.
Culture will become competitive in the future
The value of the Korean Wave civilization far exceeds that of the traditional manufacturing industry.
The Korean Wave market is 76 billion dollars in 2024 (KRW 100 trillion)
It is expected to be $143 billion (KRW 190 trillion) in 2030.

한국은 부지런한 아침의 나라

한국의 고대국가 단군조선의 이름은 아사달(阿斯達)이야.
아사(阿斯)는 아침, 달(達)은 응달 양달 하는 땅,
아침 해가 떠오르는 땅, 즉 조선(朝鮮)이지.
아리수는 아침을 여는 한강(漢江)이고.

한국인은 이른 아침에 일을 시작하지.
천성이 자연을 닮아 순리에 좇아 사는 사람들.

한국의 노래는 소리와 혼으로 부르는 종교의식,
한국의 춤은 몸과 혼으로 추는 하늘에 닿는 예술,
한국인은 행복을 불러오고 불행과 악귀를 물리치는 것이
노래와 춤이라 여기고 살아.
그래서 심금을 울리는 신녀(shaman)의 소리를 지니고 있어.
태초에 바람과 소리가 있어 사람이 살고 사랑한다고 믿지.

대한(大韓)이라는 말은 세계가 크게 하나 되자는 얘기야.

Korea Is a Diligent Morning Country

The name of Dangun Joseon, an ancient country in Korea, is Asadal(阿斯達).
Asa(阿斯) is the morning, Dal is the shady and sunny land,
It is the land where the morning sun rises, that is, Joseon.
Arisu is the Han River that opens the morning.

Koreans start working early in the morning.
People whose nature resembles nature and lives according to reason.

Korean songs are religious ceremonies sung by sound and soul.
Korean dance is the art of touching the sky with the body and soul.
Koreans live by thinking that singing and dancing bring happiness and defeat misfortune and evil spirits.
That's why it has the sound of a shaman that touches the heartstrings.
They believe that people live and love because of the wind and sound in the beginning.
The word "Daehan" means that the world should become one.

한국의 성공 배경

한국의 성공은 3E 덕분이야.
Education. 밥을 굶어도 공부해라.
Economy. 땀 흘려 노력해서 잘 살아라.
Entertainment. 즐겁게 살아라.

9천 년 동안 만들고 익혀온 고유문화를 사랑하여
K-pop, K-folk song, K-drama, K-trot,
K-movie, K-webtoon, K-food,
K-medical, K-edu, K-housing, K-game, K-heritage
K-beauty, K-language, K-fashion을 만들었지.
이제 한류 거리에는 'K뷰티 쇼핑 패스'도 생겨나고 있어.

이 모든 것의 원형은 바로
인간 세상의 공동번영을 꿈꾸고,
삶을 자연의 순리대로 살며,
나부터 온전한 인격체가 되려는 정신과 노력이야.
그것들이 문화와 놀이로 나타난 것이
한류(Hallyu),
K-culture,
K-joy야.

Background of Korea's Success

Korea's success is due to 3E.
Education. Study even if you don't eat.
Economy. Sweat and work hard to live a good life.
Entertainment. Enjoy your life.

They love unique culture that they have made and mastered for 9,000 years
K-pop, K-folk song, K-drama, K-trot,
K-movie, K-webtoon, K-food,
K-medical, K-edu, K-housing, K-game, K-heritage.
And they made K-beauty, K-language, K-fashion.
Now, "K-beauty shopping pass" is also popping up on Hallyu Street.

The prototype of all this is
Dreaming of co-prosperity in the human world,
Live your life in the order of nature,
It's the spirit and effort to become a full person from me.
The fact that they emerged as culture and play
Hallyu,
K-culture,
It's K-joy.

한국 현대사의 두 위대한 지도자

한국 현대사에는 걸출한 두 명의 위인이 있어.
이승만 대통령과 박정희 대통령이야.
이승만은 미국 프린스턴대학교 철학박사로
일제 강점기에 독립운동을 벌여 국제적으로 유명한 분이고,
상해임시정부의 초대 대통령으로 활동하였어.
1948년 대한민국을 건국하여 초대 대통령이 된 건국의
아버지야.
그는 6.25 전란으로 혼란한 대한민국을 지켜내어
자유대한민국 발전의 초석이 된 분으로
스탈린과 마오쩌둥, 김일성이 두려워한 지도자야.

박정희는 1961년 군사혁명을 단행하여
철저한 안보태세를 강화하여 북한의 재침을 막았고,
경제근대화로 대한민국 부흥을 주도한 지도자야.
박정희의 국가 근대화모델은 지금 세계 개발도상국에서
그대로 따라서 배우고 있어.
박정희의 경제발전 활동으로 한국은 민주화의 토대를 만들었고,
한국의 국민소득이 80달러(1960년)에서 2,200달러(1979년)로 증가했어.

The two great leaders of modern Korean history

There are two great men in modern Korean history.
It's President Syngman Rhee and President Park Chung-hee.
Syngman Rhee is a Ph.D. in philosophy at Princeton University.
He was famous internationally for his independence movement during the Japanese occupation.
He served as the first president of the Provisional Government of Shanghai.
He is the founding father who founded the Republic of Korea in 1948 and became the first president.
He became the cornerstone of the development of a free Korea by protecting the Republic of Korea, which was confused by the Korean War, and was feared by Stalin, Mao Zedong, and Kim Il-sung.

Park Chung-hee carried out the military revolution in 1961
It strengthened its security posture to prevent North Korea from re-invading.
He is a leader who led the revival of the Republic of Korea through economic modernization.
Park Chung-hee's national modernization model is now being learned in developing countries around the world.
Park Chung-hee's economic development activities laid the

foundation for democratization in Korea,

Korea's national income increased from $80(1960) to $2,200(1979).

President Rhee Syng-man and President Park Chung-hee,
two leaders of modern Korean history

한글(韓㖿, Hangeul) 찬가

ㄱ,ㄴ,ㄷ,ㄹ,ㅁ,ㅂ,ㅅ,ㅇ,ㅈ,ㅊ,ㅋ,ㅌ,ㅍ,ㅎ의 자음 14자
ㅏ,ㅑ,ㅓ,ㅕ,ㅗ,ㅛ,ㅜ,ㅠ,ㅡ,ㅣ의 모음 10자
한글 24자를 일주일만 배우면,
누구든 한글을 읽고 쓸 수 있지.
한글은 가장 과학적이고 배우기 쉬운 소리글자.
소리 나는 대로 적으면 글이 되고 뜻이 돼.
소리와 뜻과 글자가 하나로 표시되는 소리글.
세상에 못 쓰는 소리가 없는 세계 최고의 음성문자.
1만 1,000개의 발음을 문자로 옮길 수 있는 유일한 문자.

인공지능(AI)과 호환이 가능한 유일한 문자인 한글.
그 오묘한 입놀림 혀 놀림, 귀 놀림, 몸놀림이,
뇌에 깊고 긴 주름이 잡히듯이,
시냅스를 만들어 언어의 신화를 만들었지.
세계 문자올림픽에서 1등은 한글, 2등 인도어, 3등이 영어였어.

Hangeul (Korean letters) Psalm

14 consonants of ㄱ, ㄴ, ㄷ, ㄹ, ㅁ, ㅂ, ㅅ, ㅇ, ㅈ, ㅊ, ㅋ, ㅌ, ㅍ, ㅎ.
10 vowels of ㅏ, ㅑ, ㅓ, ㅕ, ㅗ, ㅛ, ㅜ, ㅠ, ㅡ, ㅣ.
You can learn 24 Korean letters for a week,
Anyone can read and write Korean.
The most scientific and easy-to-learn sound letter.
If you write it down as it sounds, it becomes a writing and a meaning.
A sound that displays sound, meaning, and letters as one.
The world's best Phonetic Alphabet without the sound it can't use.
The only character that can translate 11,000 pronunciations into letters.
Hangeul, the only character compatible with artificial intelligence (AI).
The subtle movement of the mouth, tongue-in-cheek, ear-in-cheek, body-in-cheek,
Just as deep and long wrinkles are formed in the brain,
They created synapses, they created the myth of language.
In the World Alphabet Olympics, the first place was Korean, the second place was Indian, and the third place was English.

한글은 세계 최고의 표음문자

세계에는 3대 발명 문자가 있어.
로마자와 중국의 한자 그리고 한국의 한글,
한글은 한국인들이 독창적으로 만들어낸 거야.
580년 전, 조선의 세종대왕과 집현전(集賢殿) 학자들이
만들었지.
한국은 독창적인 표음문자인 한글을 갖고 사는 문명국이야.
한국은 10월 9일을 '한글날'로 정해서 국경일로 삼고 있어.

CNN이 듀오링고(Duolingo)*의 조사 결과(23.1.17),
한국어는 세계 언어 중 일곱 번째로 많이 학습된 언어야.
한글을 가르치는 세종학당은 84개국에 248개,
지금까지 수료생이 70만 명이야.
<한국학>은 97개국 1,143개 대학에서 배우고 있어.
매년 한국어능력시험(TOPIK) 응시자가 68개국 33만 명.
그 합격증 갖고 한국에 유학하고, 취업도 할 수 있어.
재한(在韓) 유학생이 14만 명, 취업 외국인은 100만 명이 넘어.
이것을 코리안 드림이라고 불러.
한류를 이해하고 즐기려면 한글부터 배워야 해.
한글은 앞으로 가장 강력하고 유용한 세계어가 될 거야.

* 듀오링고(Duolingo) : 글로벌 언어학습 애플리케이션

Hangeul is the world's best phonetic alphabet

There are three major inventions in the world.
Roman characters, Chinese characters, and Korean characters.
Hangeul was originally created by Koreans.
It was created 580 years ago by King Sejong of the Joseon Dynasty and scholars of Jiphyeonjeon(集賢殿).
Korea is a civilized country that lives with Hangeul, which is an original phonetic script.
In Korea, October 9th is a national holiday called 'Hangeul Day.'

CNN reported Duolingo's findings (23.1.17),
Korean is the seventh most learned language in the world.
There are 248 King Sejong Institute that teaches Hangeul in 84 countries around the world, there have been 700,000 graduates so far.
<Korean Studies> is being taught in 1,143 universities in 97 countries.
The number of applicants who take the Test of Proficiency in Korean (TOPIK) is 330,000 in 68 countries every year.
They can study abroad in Korea with a pass certificate and get a job.
There are more than 140,000 international students in Korea and more than 1 million foreigners working in Korea.

They call this the Korean Dream.

To understand and enjoy the Korean Wave, you have to learn Korean first. Hangeul will be the most powerful and useful world language in the future.

Hunminjeongeum Reveals the fundamentals of Hangeul Creation. Hangeul was created during the reign of King Sejong, the 7th king of Joseon

K-콘텐츠의 확대

한류는 2022년에 들어 앵글을 완성했지.
BTS가 아메리칸 뮤직어워즈 등 여러 상을 받았고,
영화 <기생충>이 아카데미 작품상, 감독상, 각본상,
국제극영화상 등 4관왕을 차지했어.
<오징어게임>이 미국 TV분야 최고 상인 에미상에서
남우주연상과 감독상 등 6관왕에 올랐어.
이처럼 K팝, K영화, K드라마의 3분야에서 세계 톱을 차지했어.
한국에는 긴 역사와 문화전통 덕분에 무궁무진한 스토리가 있어.
앞으로 세계인과 함께하는 콘텐츠를 만들어낼 수 있을 거야

'한류의 M-belt'도 있어.
남아프리카공화국에서 이집트-중동-유럽으로 올라가고,
러시아와 중앙아시아 인도를 거쳐 동남아로,
중국과 몽골 일본-북미와 남미로 이어지는 형태의
영문 대문자가 바로 M자야.
한류가 세계의 주변부까지 퍼지고 있는 문화전파의 벨트이지.
세계 220개 국가에 한류의 기운이 전달되고 있다는 얘기야.
전 세계에 <한류동호회>가 1,500개,
세계의 한류 팬이 2억 명이요.
한국을 찾아오는 외국관광객이 한 해 1,000만 명이야.

Expansion of K-Contents

The Korean Wave completed the angle in 2022.
BTS won several awards including the American Music Awards,
The movie "Parasite" won four awards, including the Academy Award for Best Picture, Best Director, Best Screenplay, and Best International Drama Film.
"Squid Game" won six awards, including the Best Actor and Best Director, at the Emmy Awards, the top award in the U.S. TV field.
Like this, it topped the world in three areas : K-pop, K-movie, and K-drama.
There are endless stories in Korea because of its long history and cultural traditions.
You'll be able to create content with people around the world in the future

There's also "Hallyu's M-belt."
From South Africa to Egypt to the Middle East to Europe,
Russia, Central Asia, and India to Southeast Asia,
The capital letters in English, which are connected to China, Mongolia, Japan, North America, and South America, are the letters M.
The Korean Wave is the belt of cultural propagation that is spreading to the periphery of the world.

In other words, the Korean Wave is being delivered to 220 countries around the world.

There are 1,500 "Hallyu Clubs" around the world,

There are 200 million Korean Wave fans around the world.

There are 10 million foreign tourists coming to Korea per year.

일본 도쿄돔에서 공연중인 한국 가수들
Korean Singers Performing at Tokyo Dome in Japan

충무공 이순신 동상(忠武公李舜臣銅像, Statue of Admiral Yi Sun-sin)
Admiral Yi Sun-shin is a hero who saved Joseon by sacrificing his life in the face of a seven-year Japanese invasion in the late 16th century.

6장

노래 아리랑(我理朗)의 참뜻

아모르 파티(Amor Fati)

곤경에 빠진 나를 구하는 지혜

멍때리기의 힘

멍때리기 수련 10가지

숨비소리

지푸라기

노래 아리랑(我理朗)의 참뜻

한국에서 제일 유명한 전통 노래 아리랑은
<세계 최우수곡 선정대회>에서 82% 지지율로
가장 아름다운 곡 1위에 선정됐어요.

"아리랑 아리랑 아라리요 아리랑 고개를 넘어간다.
나를 버리고 가시는 님은 십 리도 못 가서 발병 난다."

아리랑의 참뜻은 뭘까?
'아'(我)는 참된 나(眞我)를 의미하고,
'리'(理)는 알다, 다스리다, 통한다는 뜻,
'랑'(朗)은 밝다, 즐겁다는 뜻이죠.

'참 나를 깨닫는 기쁨을 노래한 깨달음의 노래'이죠.
'아리랑 고개를 넘어간다'는 나를 찾기 위해 깨달음의 언덕,
피안(彼岸)의 언덕을 넘어간다는 뜻이죠.

The true meaning of Arirang (我理朗)

The most famous traditional song in Korea is Arirang.
With an 82% approval rating at the World's Best Song Contest
It was chosen as the most beautiful song.

"Arirang Arirang Arariyo. I'm going over Arirang Pass.
The one who abandons me gets sick in his feet because he can't even go 4km."

What is the true meaning of Arirang?
"Ah" (我) means the true me (眞我),
"Ri" (理) means knowing, governing, and communicating,
"Rang"(朗) means bright and joyful.

It's "The song of enlightenment that sings about the joy of realizing myself."
"Going Over Arirang Pass" is the hill of enlightenment to find me. It means going over the hills of Nirvana.

※ Arirang is a song that contains beautiful, mournful rhythms and lessons from an antique life.

아모르 파티 (Amor Fati)

우리는 지구와 인간을 살리는 소금별.
작지만, 보석처럼 빛이 나는 생명의 별.
빛과 사랑과 정의의 메신저.
지구와 인류가 다시 빙하시대로 돌아가지 않도록
평화와 조화가 숨 쉬는 세상이
다시는 암흑으로 바뀌지 않도록
동방의 빛으로 온 세상을 찬란하게 비추리.

사람이 뉘우치며 흘리는 눈물도 짜고,
수고하는 땀방울도 짜다는 것을 알리리라.
한 방울의 눈물 속에, 한 방울의 땀 속에
꼭꼭 숨어있는 소금 아이들
세상이 독성으로 물들어 썩지 말라고,
눈물과 땀은 소금 맛을 잃지 않느니
그 사랑의 힘으로
때로는 다이너마이트도 터뜨리고
때로는 바다에 프러포즈도 하면서
불타오르는 댄스를 출거야.
모두가 엄마 아리랑을 부를 거야.

세상의 모든 부모에게 피와 땀과 눈물을 요구하고
최초의 시작이 있던 때를 잊지 않고
그 길을 찾는 방법을 끊임없이 탐색할 거야.

꿈을 잃지 않는 삶이 행복이라는 증거를
세계의 아미(ARMY)들에게 알려 줄 거야.
한국음악을 사랑하는 팬들에게
배를 띄워 희망의 나라로 가자고 말해줄 거야
우리의 꿈, 우리의 길을 잃지 않을 거야
아니, 기어코 우리의 갈 길을 찾아내어
영원한 봄날을 그릴 거야
세상을 구원하는 일에 우리 생명을 바칠 거야

시방 삼 세대 간 시공간을 넘어
영원한 평화와 번영을 추구할 거야
정의와 진실의 화살처럼 늘 참되게 살다 갈 거야
세상을 소복소복 낙원으로 만드는
새로운 DNA가 될 거야.
그 DNA가 끊임없이 분열하여
생명을 이어가도록 빛으로 존재하자고
기도하는 마음으로 혼을 바쳐 춤추고 노래할 거야

뿌라비다(Pura Vida)!
오, 행복한 인생!
아모르 파티(Amor Fati)!
네 운명을 사랑하라!

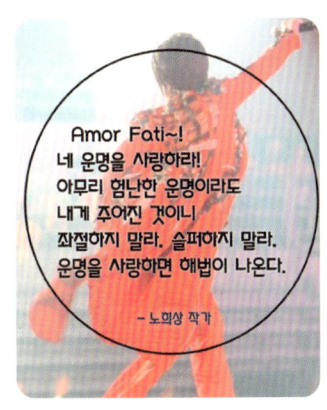

Amor Fati

We are a salt star that saves the earth and humans.
Small, but like a gem, the light is the star of life.
A messenger of light and love and justice.
Don't let the Earth and mankind go back to the Ice Age
The world where peace and harmony breathe
Don't let it go dark again
Shine the whole world brilliantly with the light of the East.
Weeping tears of repentance,

I will let you know that even sweat drops of
hard work are salty.
In one tear, in one sweat Salt kids who are hiding
Don't let the world rot because it's toxic,
Tears and sweat do not lose the taste of salt
With the power of love
Sometimes they pop dynamite
Sometimes I propose to the sea
I'm going to do a burning dance.
Everyone will sing Mom Arirang.

I want blood, sweat, and tears from every parent in the world
I won't forget the first time
I'll be constantly searching for ways to find that way.

It's the proof that life without losing your dreams is happiness

I'll let ARMY around the world know.

To the fans who love Korean music

I'm gonna set you a boat up and tell you to go to the land of hope

Our dreams, we won't lose our way

No, we're gonna find our way

I'm going to draw an eternal spring day

We're going to devote our lives to saving the world

Beyond three generations of time and space

I'm going to pursue eternal peace and prosperity

Like the arrow of justice and truth, I'm always going to live like a real life

Making the world a small paradise

It's going to be a new DNA.

The DNA is constantly breaking apart

Let's be light so that we can continue our lives

I'm going to dance and sing with all my heart in prayer

Pura Vida!

Oh, happy life!

Amor Fati!

Love your destiny!

곤경에 빠진 나를 구하는 지혜

살아가면서 위기에 처하거든 당황하지 말고,
왜 나에게 이런 불행이 왔는가 자책하지도 마.
나만이 힘들고 억울하다고 좌절하지 마.
어차피 시간은 흘러가는 거야. 막을 수는 없어.
내 안의 양심에 따라 정직하게 살면 돼.
내 가슴의 물꼬를 항상 터놓고 살면 길이 열려.
아무리 폭우가 거세도 그치지 않는 비는 없어.

나에게 불행이 오거든 하늘의 뜻이라 생각하고,
차분하고 경건하게 대하면 돼.
나에게 행복이 생기면 하늘의 선물이라 생각하고,
겸손하게 어려운 이웃을 생각하면 돼.

나에게 찾아온 슬픔이나 기쁨은 허상일 뿐이야.
힘들 땐 지금까지 걸어온 길을 돌아봐.
행복과 불행은 똑같은 질량으로 생겨나는 법,
큰 행복에 대한 욕심은 버려야 해.

여명(黎明)은 참고 노력한 자에게 오는 희망의 신호등,
이제 곧 새로운 태양이 떠오를 거야.
해야 솟아라! 해야 솟아라!
너와 나의 가슴에 맑고 고운 해야 솟아라!

Wisdom to save me in trouble

Don't panic if you're in danger in your life,
Don't blame yourself for this misfortune on me.
Don't be frustrated that I'm the only one who's tired and unfair.
Time goes by anyway. There's no stopping it.
You can live honestly according to my conscience.
If you always open up your chest, it opens up your way.
No matter how strong the downpour is, there is no rain that doesn't stop.

If misfortune comes to me, I think it's the will of heaven,
You just have to be calm and reverent.
If I have happiness, I think it's a gift from heaven,
Just be humble and think about your neighbors in need.

The sadness or joy that came to me is just an illusion.
If you're having a hard time, look back on the path you've walked so far.
Happiness and unhappiness are created in the same mass,
You have to give up your greed for great happiness.

The dawn is a traffic light of hope that comes to those who put up with it,
Soon a new sun will rise.
The sun rises! The sun rises!
The clear and beautiful sun rises in your hearts and my hearts!

멍 때리기의 힘

우리는 뭔가 채우기 위해 하루하루 허덕이며 산다.
생리적 만족, 돈과 권력, 명예, 지식과 정보, 문화적 욕구 등.
자꾸 채워나감으로써 부자가 된 것처럼 생각한다.
그런데 아무리 재주를 부려도 모든 욕구를 채울 수 없어.
내 욕구의 용량은 겨우 1배럴 통인데, 10만 배럴을 채우려 들지.
그래서 채우지 못함에 안절부절하다 분별없는 짓을 하고,
남의 것을 탐하고, 죄를 짓기도 한다.
그러나 인간의 욕구는 끝없는 것이라,
아무리 발버둥 쳐도 다 채울 수 없다는 것을 알게 되지.
나중에 깨닫는 건, 채움이란 결국 허망함이라는 것일 뿐.

삶의 과정을 통해서 하는 수행이 '멍 때리기'이다.
돈 안 드는 자기 수행 방법이다.
이 세상 모든 번뇌에서 벗어나 멍하게 앉아 생각을 비운다.
나의 복잡한 생각을 비워야 욕망이 자제된다.
그 멍때리기 방법으로 자연으로 돌아간다.
자연의 일부인 인간이 자연으로 돌아감으로써 자신을 발견한다.
'텅 빈 충만'의 경지를 경험하게 된다.
그리고 진실한 충족감을 느낀다.
멍때리기는 매우 생산적인 자기 정화의 방법이다.

The power of spacing out

We struggle day by day to fill something up.
Physiological satisfaction, money and power, honor, knowledge and information, cultural needs, etc.
We think we've become rich by constantly filling up.
But no amount of dexterity can satisfy all the needs.
The capacity of my needs is only one barrel, and I'm going to fill 100,000 barrels.
Therefore, I am restless because I cannot fill it, and I do senseless things, and I also covet other people's things, and commit a crime.
But human needs are endless.
No matter how hard you struggle, you find that you can't fill it all up.
What you realize later is that filling is, after all, vain.

The practice through the process of life is 'spacing out.'
It's a self-fulfilling method that doesn't cost money.
I sit blankly away from all the anguish in the world and empty my thoughts.
I have to empty my complicated thoughts to control my desire.
Back to nature in that way of spacing out.
Humans, part of nature, find themselves by returning to nature.
You experience the state of 'empty fullness.'
And you feel a real sense of fulfillment.
Spacing out is a very productive method of self-purification.

멍때리기* 수련 10가지

'불멍'은 뜨겁게 타오르는 불길을 보면서 욕망을 태워 없애는 것.
'물멍'은 소낙비, 분수대, 강물을 보며 자신의 사악함을 씻는 것.
'설(雪)멍'은 내리는 눈을 바라보며 자신의 영혼을 정화하는 것.
'풍(風)멍'은 각종 바람에 자신의 욕망을 실어보내는 것.
'갯멍'은 썰물 후에 드러난 질퍽한 개펄에 자신을 이입시키는 것.
'향(香)멍'은 향기 나는 물질을 불피워놓고 마음의 안정을 얻어
욕망을 자제시키는 것.
'태양멍'은 뜨겁게 내리쬐는 태양 아래에 몸을 드러내어 병든 몸을
치유하는 것.
'별(星)멍'은 밤하늘의 별을 바라보며 사후에 내가 갈 곳을
더듬어보는 영혼의 순행.
'글멍'은 불경, 논어, 성경, 철학자, 소설에서 뽑은 중요한 구절을
필사하여 마음을 수행하는 것.

홍대로(弘大路)에 가면 멍때리기 좋은 곳이 많다.
가로수길 가의 벤치도 좋고,
수많은 3층, 4층의 카페 창가도 좋다.
사람들이 조용히 거니는 골목의 중간쯤도 좋다.
작은 속닥거림이 찰랑대는 물결처럼 들리는 흐름 속에,
내 눈과 가슴과 마음을 떠나보내는 '류(流)멍'도 좋다.
내 몸과 마음의 정화(淨化)를 연습하는 곳이 홍대로이다.
그것은 큰 바다에서 다시 만나기 위한 구원의 의식이다.

* 아무 생각 없이 멍하게 있으면서 자신을 돌아보는 수행 방법이다. 불이 타오르는 것을
가만히 바라보는 것을 '불멍'이라고 한다.

10 Spacing Out(Mung*) exercises

'Bulmung' is about burning away desire while watching a hot fire.

'Mulmung' means washing one's wickedness while looking at the snowfalls, fountains, and rivers.

'Snowmung' means purifying one's soul while looking at the falling snow.

'Windmung' is to send one's desire to various winds.

'Gatmung' is about transferring oneself to the muddy tidal flats revealed after low tide.

'ScentedMung' is about burning fragrant substances and controlling desires by gaining peace of mind.

'Sunmung' is the healing of a sick body by revealing itself under the hot sun.

'Byeolmung' is a journey of the soul looking at the stars in the night sky and looking for a place to go after death.

'Geulmung' is the transcription of important passages selected from Buddhist scriptures, Analects, Bibles, Philosophers, and novels to carry out the mind.

If you go to Hongdae-ro, there are many good places to space out. The benches along Garosu-gil are good,
Numerous cafe windows on the 3rd and 4th floors are also good.

The middle of the alley where people walk quietly is also good.
In a flow that sounds like a wave of tiny whispering
I also like 'RyuMung' that sends my eyes, heart, and heart away.
Hongik University is the place where I practice my body and mind.
It is a ritual of salvation to meet again in the great sea.

There are more and more types of spacing out.

* It's a practice method of looking back on yourself while spacing out without thinking. For example, Watching a fire burn is called a 'Bul Mung'

숨비소리

제주도 바닷가 올레길을 걷다 보면,
물질하고 올라온 해녀들의 거친 숨소리를 듣는다.
'호오이~~~ 호오이~~~'
'휘이이~~~ 휘이이~~~'
얼마나 숨이 가빴으면 그렇게 휘파람 소리를 내면서,
몸속의 이산화탄소를 내뱉고 산소를 들이마실까?
그 절규와 같은 자연의 본능 소리를 '숨비소리'라 한다.
숨이 코에까지 올라 찼다는 이야기이다.

해녀가 깊은 물 속에 들어가 숨을 멈추고 물질하는 시간은
생과 사가 오가는 운명을 가르는 기적적인 호흡이다.

해녀가 물질하고 올라오다가 값비싼 해물을 보면,
다시 그것을 채취하고 싶은 욕심이 생긴단다.
하지만 다시 내려갔다가는 생명을 잃고 만다.
그래서 일단 수면 위로 올라와 숨을 고르고 다시 내려간다.
우리는 살다가 절박한 상황이 되면 초인적인 힘을 발휘한다.
그렇다 해도 숨이 멎을 정도로 과욕을 부리면 안 된다.
아무리 돈이 중하다 해도 분수를 넘으면 삶을 망친다.
해녀의 '숨비소리'처럼 우리에게도 '양심의 소리'가 있다.
한류 문명은 인류에게 주는 적절한 '숨비소리'이다.

The sound of Breath ratio

If you walk along the Olle trail by the sea of Jeju Island,
We hear the harsh breathing of Haenyeo who came up with the material.
"Hooray~" "Hui~Hui~"
How short of breath she must have been, whistling like that,
Does she exhale carbon dioxide in her body and breathe in oxygen?
The sound of nature's instinct, such as the scream, is called 'breath sound.'
It is said that her breath was up to her nose.

The time when a Haenyeo enters deep water, stops breathing, and materializes is a miraculous breath that separates the fate of life and death.

When a Haenyeo comes up with a substance and sees expensive seafood, she has a desire to collect it again.
But when she goes down again, she loses her life. So she comes up to the surface, takes a breath, and goes down again.
We use superhuman strength when we are in desperate situations in our lives. Even so, you shouldn't over-greed to the point where you can't take your breath away.

No matter how important money is, it ruins your life if you exceed your means. Just like Haenyeo's 'the sound of Breath ratio.'
The Korean Wave civilization is an appropriate 'breathing sound' given to mankind.

해녀는 연해에서 해조류와 어패류를 채취하는 여자 다이버이다. 제주도가 그녀들의 본거지이다.
Haenyeo is a female diver who collects seaweed, fish, and shellfish from the coastal waters. Jeju Island is their home.
(국내_대한민국_6348, 한국저작권위원회, 공유마당, CC BY)

지푸라기

한 줌의 지푸라기라고 우습게 보지 마라
지푸라기는 천지의 기운을 머금고 자란 까닭에
고고한 선비의 인품,
어진 심청이의 한없는 효심을 지녔고,
쌀을 지어 인간에게 바치는 생명 구원의 표상이다

그는 온몸을 태워 구들장을 덥히고,
온몸으로 홍어를 끌어안고 삭히며,
황토와 궁합이 맞아 흙벽돌을 만들고,
초가지붕의 이엉이 되어 추위와 비를 막아주며,
소에게는 귀한 생명의 여물이 된다.
타서 재가 되면 질소비료가 되어 땅의 음식이 된다.

그리고 절망에 빠져 죽음을 생각하는 사람에게
나를 잡고 살아나라고 용수철 같은 희망의 손을 내민다

한 줌 지푸라기만도 못한 사람들아!
길을 걷다가 지푸라기를 만나거든
고맙다고 말해주라.
제발 늙거든 검불이라도 되어
나그네 사랑방의 아궁이라도 덥혀주려마.

Straws

Don't look down on a handful of straws
Straws are grown with the energy of heaven and earth
the character of a noble scholar,
He has the infinite filial piety of a young Simcheong*,
It is a symbol of the salvation of life by making rice and giving it to humans.

He burns his whole body to heat up the bowels,
With his whole body, he embraced the big stingray and fermented it,
It goes well with loess, so it makes soil bricks.
It becomes a roof made of straw, which protects against cold and rain, It is a precious waste of life for cows.
When burned, it becomes nitrogen fertilizer and becomes food on the ground.

And to someone who thinks of dying in despair
Put out a springy hand of hope to catch me

Those of you who are not even a handful!
When you're walking down the street, you meet straws
Please say thank you.

Please, if you get old, you'll be a dirty straw

You're going to heat up the furnace of a traveler's accommodation.

지푸라기
Straw left over after harvesting rice

* Simcheong : In a traditional fairy tale, a filial daughter who opened the eyes of a blind father by throwing her life into the sea

훈민정음(訓民正音, Hunminjeongeum)은 한글(Hangeul, Korean alphabet)의 제정과 원리를 선언한 창조문자이다.
Hunminjeongeum is a creative script that proclaims the establishment and principle of Hangeul(Korean alphabet).

부록 / 한글 시 감상

들꽃 인생
사랑의 힘
아내의 기도
사당역 나그네

한글시 감상 / 노 단 지음

들꽃 인생

길가에 핀 한 송이 이름 모를 꽃
들꽃이라 불리지만, 나의 이름은 사랑꽃
아리랑의 전설을 노래하며
세찬 폭풍우도 견뎌내고 살아온 꽃
바람과 햇빛이 친구였어요.

뜨거운 폭염이 벼를 익히고,
천둥 번개가 쳐야 과일이 익는 법이라고,
살면서 힘들지 않은 사람은 없으며,
슬픔은 하늘의 선물이라고 위로하던
제비꽃 민들레꽃은 나의 친구였어요.

슬프고 배고파도 웃음과 노래로
힘들어하는 친구들을 위로하며 살아왔지.
하늘은 견딜 수 있을 만큼의 고난을 준다고
참고 기다리면 복이 찾아온다 말하던,
비와 눈은 나의 친구였어요.

Enjoying Korean poetry/ written by Rohdan

A life like a wild flower

An unknown flower on the side of the road
It is called wild flower, but my name is love flower
Singing the legend of Arirang
A flower that has survived a strong storm
The wind and the sun were friends.

Hot heat waves ripen rice,
The fruit ripens only when thunder and lightning strike,
There's no one who doesn't have a hard time in their lives,
It was consoled that grief is a gift from heaven
Violet Dandelion was my friend.

Even if you're sad and hungry, with laughter and singing
I've lived comforting my friends who are struggling.
The sky gives you enough hardship to endure
If you put up with it and wait, you'll be blessed,
Rain and snow were my friends.

사랑의 힘

우리는 사랑의 힘으로 거친 인생을 산다.
사랑이란 내 삶의 빛이요 식량이다.
사랑은 살아서 누릴 수 있는 최고의 가치,
사랑은 나를 구원하는 신앙같은 것,
사랑을 원하기 전에 내가 먼저 사랑을 주자.
사랑하는 사람이 있어 그리워하는 건 축복이다.

네 주위에는 온통 사랑을 갈구하는 것뿐이야.
내 나라와 내 가족, 친구들,
나의 일터와 동료들과 손님들,
내가 키우는 반려동물, 꽃과 나무, 금붕어,
내가 믿는 종교와 신앙,
내가 쓰는 일기와 내가 그리는 그림 한 점,
내가 부르는 노래와 내가 만드는 음식,
나의 눈물과 연민의 한숨까지
내 작은 생각의 조각조차 사랑일 뿐이지.

당신이 진정 사랑에 목이 마르다면
당신의 몸과 마음부터 사랑하라.
그리고 지치고 힘든 이웃을 사랑하라.
그 기운은 몇 천 배의 에너지로 그대에게 돌아올 것이다.

The Power of Love

We live rough lives with the power of love.
Love is the light of my life and food.
Love is the best value I can enjoy in my life,
Love is like a faith that saves me,
Let me give you love first before anyone wants it.
It's a blessing to miss someone you love.

All around you is longing for love.
My country, my family, my friends,
My workplace, colleagues and guests,
My pet, flowers and trees, goldfish,
The religion and the faith I believe in,
My diary and a picture I draw,
The song I sing and the food I make,
Even my tears and sighs of compassion
Even a small piece of my thought is just love.

If you're really thirsty for love
Love your body and heart first.
And love your tired and struggling neighbor.
The energy will return to you with thousands of times more energy.

아내의 기도

아내는 매일 새벽마다
정화수를 흰 대접에 떠 놓고
성냥으로 촛불을 켠다
깨끗한 소금을 옴팍 접시에 담고
그 위에 향불 세 개를 꽂은 뒤
'삼신랑' '삼신랑'
두 손을 합장하며 칠성신에게 빈다
나라와 가족을 위해 소원을 빈다

어느새 오십 년을 빌다 보니
우리 집에서 가장 경건한 예배 시간이다
나는 뒷방에 앉아 글을 쓰면서
그 아내의 음성에 실린 향내를 귀로 맡는다
경건한 마음으로 삶의 엄숙함과 사랑의 뜻을 흡입한다
그리고 수 만 년 이어 내려온
한민족의 거룩한 종교가
백성의 피에 흐르고 있음을 느낀다.

* 이 글은 노단이 시인으로 등단할 때 추천받은 시이다.

A Wife's Prayer

Every morning, every dawn, my wife
Put the purified water in a white bowl
light a candle with a match
Put clean salt in a deep-cut plate
After putting three incense burners on top of it
"Three Beloved." "Three Beloved."
Put her hands together and pray to the Seven Saints
She wishs for country and family

My wife has been praying for 50 years
It's the most reverent time of worship in my house
I sat in the back room and wrote
I hear the scent of the wife's voice
Inhale the solemnity of life and the will of love with reverence
And it's been tens of thousands of years
the holy religion of the Korean people
I feel that it is in the blood of the people.

* This is a poem recommended when Rohdan debuted as a poet.

사당역 나그네

서울 지하철 2, 4호선 사당역
환승 다문화 마당에 음악이 흐른다

페루에서 온 잉카의 후손들이
치렁치렁한 색색의 옷, 긴 생머리로
화산재 내음 가득 담은 플루트를 연주한다
파랑새 날개매듭에 비 내리듯 구슬픈 가락이
정열의 마그마(Magma)에 풀어져
휘휘 거리며 내 심장과 귀 입맛을 당긴다

홀리듯 서 있던 나는 그 가락 속에
내 슬픔 한 덩어리를 버무려 넣었다
백 포기 김장하는 마음으로
노래의 배춧잎 속에 시(詩)의 양념을 발라주었다.

* 이 글은 노단이 시인으로 등단할 때 추천받은 시이다.

Sadang Station Traveler

Sadang Station on Seoul Subway Lines 2 and 4
Music flows in the multicultural yard of the transfer

The descendants of Incas from Peru
Clothes of various colors, long hair
play a flute full of volcanic ash
The sad melody of the blue bird's wing knot as if it were raining
It's released by the magma of passion
Whistling, pulling my heart and my ear palate

I was standing like I was possessed, in that rhythm
I mixed up a piece of my sadness
With the heart of making kimchi for 100 heads of cabbage
The cabbage leaves of the song were seasoned with poetry.

* This is a poem recommended when Rohdan debuted as a poet.

'무료글꼴, 강원특별자치도 속초시, 속초바다 손글씨체'
'무료글꼴, 경기도 동두천시, 소요단풍체'
'무료글꼴, 강원특별자치도, 강원교육모두'
'무료글꼴, 서울특별시, 서울한강체'
'T&ab신영복체 '박윤정앤타이포랩, 공유마당, OFL'